GW01161382

THE LAW OF SEWERS AND DRAINS

Other works by J. F. Garner:
Local Land Charges
Law of Allotments
Law of Public Cleansing
Civic Ceremonial
Administrative Law   (*with* R. K. Crow, B.Sc.):
Clean Air, Law and Practice

The Law of
Sewers and Drains

under the Public Health Acts

by

J. F. Garner, LL.D.

Solicitor

*   *   *

SIXTH EDITION

*   *   *

"The truth is that the whole of our sanitary legislation is in a state which I hardly like to characterise in the language that naturally suggests itself; and the attempt to extract from the various details of the legislation a set of harmonious principles, always underlying the specific provisions, is, I am afraid, futile"—the late Mr Justice Wills, in 1896.

*   *   *

LONDON:
Printed and Published by
SHAW & SONS LTD.,
Shaway House,
Lower Sydenham, SE26 5AE
1981

First Edition.	*Published* -	-	-	- June, 1950
	Reprinted -	-	- March, 1954.
Second Edition.	*Published* -	-	- March, 1960.
Third Edition.	*Published* -	- November, 1962.
	Reprinted -	- November, 1965.
Fourth Edition.	*Published* -	-	- January, 1969.
	Reprinted -	- November, 1971.
Fifth Edition.	*Published* -	-	- January, 1975.
	Reprinted -	- September, 1976.
Sixth Edition.	*Published* -	-	- March, 1981.

ISBN 07219 0581 1

Preface to the Sixth Edition

I HAVE said in earlier editions that the law of public health continues to fail to hit the head-lines—and this remains true.but it is unfortunate that the statutory provisions on such "mundane" subjects as those with which this book is concerned remain so complicated and so dependent on Victorian legislation. And it is also most unfortunate that the reorganisation of local government made the law even more complicated. As a result of the Local Government Act 1972 and the Water Act 1973, we now have the substantive provisions of our sanitary legislation divided between the district councils (and London boroughs) on the one hand, and the mammoth (ten only) regional water authorities on the other.[1] The Control of Pollution Act 1974, though in many respects most welcome, has further complicated the story by revising the law relating to the conservancy services, and the prevention of water pollution (and the drainage of trade effluents in particular). Unfortunately this Act is still not fully in force, in spite of Government promises, but in the text of this edition, the Act is assumed to be fully in force.

There have been many detailed amendments in legislation since the last edition, and several cases of importance; these have been incorporated in the text which intends to state the law as it was on 1st July 1980.

J. F. G.

Nottingham.

---

[1] *See* Appendix, *post*, page 188.

Preface to the First Edition

IT is the purpose of this work to endeavour to bring some degree of order into chaos, and to attempt to achieve what was described by Mr.Justice Wills, over 50 years ago,[1] as "futile," namely to extract from our sanitary legislation a set of harmonious principles. The writer is not rash enough to suggest that such principles have in fact been extracted in the pages that follow, but if this book results in illuminating to any extent what is one of the darkest patches of our statute law, it is considered that the main object of the book will have been achieved. In endeavouring to attain this objective, the author has been greatly assisted by that indispensable friend, "Lumley's Public Health". Unfortunately the assistance of the Legislature, who had the opportunity of abolishing such oddities as "single private drains" in 1936, has not been so extensive. The law relating to future sewers and drains was considerably simplified by the Public Health Act, 1936, but the status of pre-1937 sewers and drains was left to be determined in accordance with the earlier, unsatisfactory, legislation.

The law relating to sewers and drains is commonly regarded as referring to the relevant provisions of the Public Health Acts, and it is so understood in the present work. For this reason therefore, incidental discussion only is included on the allied subject of land drainage, but some comment has been included on the topic of the prevention of river pollution.

---

[1] *See* quotation on the title-page of the present work, taken from Wills, J.'s judgment in *Bradford v.Eastbourne Corporation,* [1896] 2 Q.B. 205.

The law relating to the Metropolis,[1] being of a very specialised nature, is not here dealt with, nor is there any discussion of the law of Scotland or of Northern Ireland.

References are included throughout to the copyright forms of Shaw and Sons Ltd. Specimen forms will gladly be supplied on request.

The law is stated in this book as it was on 1st June, 1950.

J. F. G.

Bognor Regis.

---

[1] Since 1963, this term should be understood as referring to the area of the former L.C.C.; "inner London".

Table of Contents

Abbreviations

(except where the contrary appears).

The Secretary of State	*means* the Secretary of State for the Environment, and, in Wales, the Secretary of State for Wales, and their predecessors in title (*see post*, p. 7).
The local authority	*means* the council of a metropolitan *or* non-metropolitan district *or* the council of a London Borough and the predecessor of such a council, or the Common Council of the City of London, as explained in Chapter 1 (*see post*, p. 6).
The water authority	*means* the regional water authority or the Welsh National Water Development Authority (*see* Water Act 1973, s. 2) for the area.
The 1875 Act ...	*means* the Public Health Act, 1875.
The 1936 Act ...	*means* the Public Health Act, 1936, and references to "the Act" or to sections alone, are to this statute.
The 1961 Act ...	*means* the Public Health Act, 1961.
The 1973 Act ...	*means* the Water Act, 1973.
The 1974 Act ...	*means* the Control of Pollution Act, 1974.

Table of Statutes

List of Statutory Instruments

Table of Cases

A

B

PAGE

The Law of
Sewers and Drains

CHAPTER 1

INTRODUCTORY—DEFINITIONS

1. SEWERS AND DRAINS.

In order that the subject matter of this book may be defined, it is first important to appreciate—so far as this is humanly possible—what the law of England understands by the terms "sewer" and "drain".

Common Law.

At common law the terms had no specialised meaning,[1] and were used in their ordinary everyday sense as signifying a conduit or channel for the carrying off of surface water, sewage or faecal matter, and a "sewer" was understood to signify, in general, a large drain, or a public drain. Under the Public Health Act, 1848, the first substantial contribution made by the Legislature to our sanitary legislation, the word "drain" was used to mean a passage for sewage from a single building, and the word "sewer" extended to any system of drainage not being a drain as so defined.[2]

Statute.

The Public Health Act, 1875, also had its own definitions of these terms, but these are no longer in operation, except where it may be necessary to refer to

---

[1] In Tudor times the "Commissioners of Sewers" were established by statute to regulate land drainage, especially in the Fens. Here sewers were used to signify land drains rather than the modern conduits for sewage. In "*Callis on Sewers*", it was said (at p. 80) that "a sewer is a fresh water trench compassed on both sides with a bank, and is a small current or little river".

[2] Public Health Act, 1848, s. 2; *Sutton v. Norwich Corporation* (1858), 27 L.J. Ch. 739.

[1]

the provisions of the earlier legislation.[1] The statute in force at the present day is the Public Health Act, 1936,[2] which, by section 343 (1) thereof, defines these expressions as follows:

> " 'drain' means a drain used for the drainage of one building or of any buildings or yards appurtenant to buildings within the same curtilage.[3]"

> "sewer" is not defined expressly, but in the section referred to, it is provided that the term shall "not include a drain as defined in this section[4] but, save as aforesaid, includes all sewers and drains used for the drainage of buildings and yards appurtenant to buildings."

The term "public sewer", is defined by section 20 of the 1936 Act (as amended by the Water Act 1973), and by section 343 (1), *ibid.*, a "private sewer" is any sewer which is not a public sewer. The distinction between public and private sewers is of vital importance in this branch of the law, as explained in Chapter 2, *post.*

It is therefore a basic principle of both sewers and drains, as understood in the Public Health Acts, that they should be designed (or used) to drain buildings and constructed objects such as roads, as distinct from land itself. In applying the above definitions, judicial interpretation has been of assistance to some extent. It is reasonably clear that the nature of the effluent is not the sole determining factor as to whether a particular channel is a drain or a sewer, for a channel may

---

[1] *See post*, Chap. 2, p. 11.

[2] This is still the principal Act though now amended, so far as its administration is concerned, by the Water Act 1973; some sections of the former Public Health Acts remain in force, and since 1936, the Public Health (Drainage of Trade Premises) Act, 1937 and the Public Health Act, 1961, have been passed.

[3] *See post*, Chap. 2, p. 13.

[4] A connection leading from a public sewer to the curtilage of a single building (sometimes described as a "lateral") is therefore a drain, not a public sewer, even if it has been laid by the local authority *see post*, Chap. 2, p. 16, and Chap. 9, *post*, p. 124.

be a sewer although it carries no sewage or foul matter and though its contents consists solely of innocuous surface drainage.[1] The channel in question need not necessarily be of artificial construction to have become a sewer in law, although a natural stream cannot normally be a sewer. "It is clear, I think, that generally speaking, the beds and banks of natural rivers and streams are not sewers within the term as used in the Act of 1875. . . To prevent misconception I will add that no doubt there are circumstances in which the bed and banks of what was once a natural stream might, prior to the Act of 1875, have become substantially nothing but a channel for sewage".[2] The combined effect of section 17 of the 1875 Act[3] and section 3 of the Rivers Pollution Prevention Act, 1876,[4] was, however, to prevent any further natural streams from becoming sewers by the discharge of sewage into them.[5]

It is also clear that the expression "used for" the drainage of buildings, etc., in the above definition, is to be understood as distinguishing such a sewer from a line of pipes "used for the drainage of land or roads or other things"; a sewer designed for the drainage of buildings does not cease to be a sewer for the purposes

---

[1] *Falconar v. South Shields Corporation* (1895), 11 T.L.R. 223. It is very largely a question of degree and of fact.

[2] *Per* Lord Maugham, in *George Legge & Son v. Wenlock Corporation* [1938] A.C. 204.

[3] Now replaced by s. 30 of the 1936 Act; the 1876 Act was replaced by the Rivers (Prevention of Pollution) Act, 1951, itself now replaced by the Control of Pollution Act, 1974, when in force.

[4] The 1876 Act has now been repealed, and a suitably treated effluent from a water authority sewerage system may be discharged into a natural watercourse subject to Ministerial regulations made under s. 55 of the Control of Pollution Act, 1974. This cannot, however, have the effect of converting the watercourse into a sewer.

[5] *George Legge & Son v. Wenlock Corporation, supra.*

of the 1936 Act if without reconstruction it is not used at all.[1]

On general principles, a natural underground watercourse which had been piped by the owners of the land through which it flowed, was held not to be a sewer,[2] and a drain which carried off only rain water from the roofs of a house, was held to be a drain within the meaning of the Act of 1875.[3] Highway drains also come within the strict definition of the term "sewer", but these, and land drains, have received special attention from Parliament.[4]

Gutters and fall pipes are probably not drains in law, and almost certainly are not sewers, even if they serve more than one premises. The primary meaning of both terms as used in the statute is that of ordinary usage, which would preclude the words being used so artificially as to include objects of this kind.

Lines of Pipes as Sewers.

It has also been said that a sewer must cause the effluent to flow from one place to another; in the meaning used in the Act of 1875 (and, it is submitted, of 1936), it "must be in some form a line of flow by which sewage or water of some kind, such as would be conveyed by a sewer, should be taken from a point to a point and then discharged. It must have a *terminus a*

---

[1] *Per* Stamp, J., in *Blackdown Properties Ltd. v. Minister of Housing and Local Government* [1965] 2 All E.R. 345, at p. 348. An underground culvert originally constructed by a canal company for the purpose of draining land was not a sewer, but when in 1867 sewers were connected to it, the nature of its use was changed, and it thereupon became a sewer and vested in the predecessor of the local authority as a public sewer (and is now, presumably, vested in the water authority): *see Leigh Corporation v. British Waterways Board* (1969) 67 L.G.R. 341.

[2] *Shepherd v. Croft,* [1911] 1 Ch. 521.

[3] *Ferrand v. Hallas Land & Building Co.,* [1893] 2 Q.B. 135, *per* Smith, L.J., and *Silles v. Fulham Corporation,* [1903] 1 K.B. 829 the fact that a particular sewer does not carry any sewage but only rain water, is immaterial.

[4] Land drains are regarded as being outside the scope of this work. As to highway drains, *see* Chap. 6, *post*, p. 91.

quo and a *terminus ad quem*".[1] A line of pipes terminating in a cesspool appears, therefore, not to be a sewer within the meaning of the 1875 Act,[2] nor is a line of pipes which has no proper outfall[3] and a conduit linking two cesspools is also not a sewer.[4] A cesspool or storage tank is not part of the sewer, unless it is really a mere catchpit from which an overflow pipe runs to a sewer or other proper outfall.[5] The mere fact that a particular outfall is not satisfactory or may cause a nuisance, does not prevent the line of pipes draining thereto from being a sewer in law, and vesting in the local authority under the 1875 Act.[6]

On the other hand, a pumping main or trunk sewer is none the less a sewer, and in most circumstances will also be a public sewer.

Subject to the above observations, the terms "sewer" and "drain" must be interpreted in accordance with the ordinary or dictionary meaning[7] of the expressions with which this chapter opened.

---

[1] *Per* Buckley, L.J., in *Pakenham v. Ticehurst R.D.C.* (1903), 67 J.P. 448.

[2] *Meader v. West Cowes Local Board*, [1892] 3 Ch. 18, and *Butt v. Snow* (1903), 67 J.P. 454. It is doubtful, however, if the principle herein applied relates to a case where a drainage system, terminating in private drainage "works," has been approved by the local authority as being initially satisfactory. Thus, a conduit ending in tanks from which the effluent was raised by mechanical means and then discharged, all of which had been constructed by a private individual and approved by the local authority, was held to be a sewer *Attorney-General v. Peacock*, [1926] Ch. 241.

[3] *Per* Maugham, J. *(obiter)*, in *Clark v. Epsom R.D.C.*, [1929] 1 Ch. 287.

[4] *Button v. Tottenham U.D.C.*, (1898), 62 J.P. 423.

[5] *Pakenham v. Ticehurst R.D.C.*, *supra*.

[6] *Clark v. Epsom R.D.C.*, *supra*, and *post*, Chap. 2. On the above authorities, it seems that a drain, serving any number of buildings, whether or not within the same curtilage, which discharges into a cesspool or cesspit (not being a mere catchpit), is not capable of being a public sewer within the provisions discussed in Chap. 2, *post*, p. 11, *et seq.* For the purposes of Part II of the 1936 Act *(i.e., ss.* 14 to 90, dealing with "Sanitation and Buildings"), "any reference to a drain or to a sewer shall be construed as including a reference to any manholes, ventilating shafts, pumps or other accessories belonging to that drain or sewer"; 1936 Act, s. 90 (4).

[7] "In the absence of any judicial guidance or authority, dictionaries can be consulted," to assist in the construction of a statute, said Asquith, J., in *Kerr v. Kennedy*, [1942] 1 K.B. 409 (and *see Maxwell on the Interpretation of Statutes*, 10th edn., p. 32).

Thus, on the following diagram, the surface water drain taking rain water from houses 1, 2 and 3 to the soakway at point X on A's property is not a sewer but a drain,[1] whereas the foul drain leading to the stream at point Y, is a sewer **from** point B.

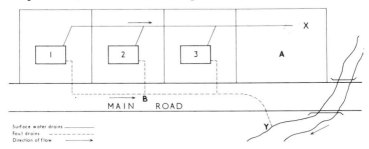

Surface water drains ——————
Foul drains   — — — — — — —
Direction of flow   ——————→

2. LOCAL AUTHORITIES.

The term "local authority" as used in the 1936 Act, and hereafter in this book, means the council of a district established under the Local Government Act, 1972, a London Borough council, the Common Council of the City of London, and also their predecessors the borough, urban and rural district councils, which had the functions of the urban and rural sanitary authorities under the 1875 Act (*see* sections 4 and 5 of that Act).[2] In central London, that is, the area formerly governed by the London County Council, the Public Health Acts apply only with modifications: *see* 1963 Act, Parts V and VI. Local authorities still have drainage and other public health functions in their own right, but as from 1st April 1974, their sewage and sewage disposal functions[3] were transferred to the water authorities[4] con-

---

[1] And therefore it cannot be a *public* sewer (see Chapter 2, *post*), even if it was constructed *before* 1937.

[2] Act of 1936, s. 1.

[3] Under s. 15 of the Water Act, 1973, agency arrangements may be made for local authorities to carry out the sewerage (but not sewage disposal) functions of water authorities Act of 1973, s. 15.

[4] Of which there are ten, including the Welsh National Water Development Authority: Water Act, 1973, s. 2.

stituted under the Water Act 1973. Public sewers also vested in the water authorities as from the same date. Except in so far as duties remain with local authorities, it is the duty of the water authority to enforce generally the provisions of the 1936 Act (as amended) relating to sewers and drains (*inter alia*), subject, in some instances, to the supervision of the Secretary of State. The division of functions between local authorities and water authorities is shown in the Appendix, *post*, page 188.

Under section 34 of the New Towns Act, 1965, the Secretary of State can confer the powers of a water authority under s. 15 of the 1936 Act on a new town development corporation for the purpose of the sewerage of the area designated as the site of a new town. When the development corporation is wound up, the sewers and works so constructed may be transferred to the water authority and not to the New Towns Commission (New Towns Act, 1965, s. 40, as amended by the Water Act 1973).[1]

3. THE CENTRAL AUTHORITY.

Under the Ministry of Health Act, 1919, the powers and duties of the former Local Government Board were transferred to the Minister of Health thereby established, which Minister was charged expressly with the execution of "all such steps as may be desirable to secure the preparation, effective carrying out and co-ordination of measures conducive to the health of the people".[2]

These functions, so far as they related to the Public Health and related Acts, were transferred to Ministers of various titles throughout the years, but since 1970

---

[1] This section has not been amended by the New Towns (Amendment) Act 1976, but presumably sewerage rights will not pass to a local authority under a transfer scheme made under that Act.
[2] Ministry of Health Act, 1919, s. 2.

have been vested in the Secretary of State for the Environment, and, in Wales, the Secretary of State for Wales (herein referred to as "the Secretary of State").

The Secretary of State is therefore the central government department responsible for the general supervision of the work of local and water authorities on matters of public health in general and sewers and drains in particular.

Complaints to the effect that a local or water authority have made default in discharging any of their functions under the 1936 Act, may be made to the Secretary of State,[1] who may then hold a local inquiry into the matter.[2] Where such an inquiry is held the procedure of s. 250 of the Local Government Act, 1972 will apply, and the inquiry will be subject to the general supervision of the Council on Tribunals (Tribunals and Inquiries (Discretionary Inquiries) Order 1975 (S.I., 1975, No. 1377), made under the Tribunals and Inquiries Act, 1971).

If the Secretary of State so decides, as a result of such inquiry or otherwise, he may make a "default order", which he may enforce (if necessary) by *mandamus* or otherwise, or by transferring the statutory functions of the authority in default to the appropriate county council (in the case of a defaulting district council), or to himself.[3]

Default powers of the Secretary of State are, however, but rarely used, and then only in extreme cases. In practice, day to day supervision (which is perhaps not as close in this sphere as is central governmental control over some other local government services) is

---

[1] Act of 1936, s. 322.
[2] *Ibid.*; where a complaint may be laid the jurisdiction of the courts is normally excluded. *See* Chap. 3, *post*, p. 32.
[3] For the consequences of such a transfer of functions, *see* ss. 323 and 324 of the 1936 Act.

exercised by the Secretary of State by the following methods:

(a) Control of finance.

Loans for capital expenditure required by the authority may be raised only with the sanction of the Secretary of State.[1] The Secretary of State in practice is able to ensure that this requirement is observed through the medium of the district auditors, who audit the great majority of local government accounts.[2]

(b) Local Inquiries.

The Secretary of State may decide to hold a local inquiry in a variety of circumstances in particular where he deems if advisable that a local inquiry should be held "in relation to any matter concerning the public health in any place" (1936 Act, s. 318), where a complaint has been made under section 322 *ibid.*, (above), or where a local authority has made application for the sanction of the Secretary of State to raise a loan. The procedure regulating such inquiries is governed by section 250 of the Local Government Act, 1972 (and *see* p. 8).

(c) Confirmation of byelaws.

Byelaws made by a local authority under the 1936 Act[3] are not operative unless and until the same have been confirmed by the Secretary of State.[4] This rule also applies to byelaws made by a water authority, for example, as to the use of a river by an unregistered vessel, under s. 48 of the Control of Pollution Act 1974.[5]

---

[1] Local Government Act, 1972, s. 172 and Schedule 13.
[2] *See* ss. 154–167 of the Local Government Act, 1972.
[3] The power to make building byelaws was repealed by the Public Health Act, 1961, and the Secretary of State has made building regulations applicable to he whole country *see* Building Regulations, 1976.
[4] 1936 Act, s 312. The procedure for confirmation of byelaws must follow that prescribed by ss. 235–238 of the Local Government Act, 1972.
[5] And *see* Water Act 1973, s. 36 (3) and Schedule 7, Part II.

CHAPTER 2

OWNERSHIP OF SEWERS

1. INTRODUCTORY.

The question whether a particular sewer belongs to a private individual or to the water authority, is one of major importance, in view of the provisions of section 23 of the 1936 Act as amended by s. 14 of the Water Act 1973, which imposes a positive duty on water authorities to "maintain, cleanse and empty," all public sewers vested in them.[1] Moreover, the powers entrusted to water authorities in respect of sewers by the 1936 Act and its predecessors, are, in general, exercisable in respect only of "public sewers vested in them".[2] The owners of private sewers have certain common law and statutory liabilities in respect thereof; but if they can repudiate ownership, they will be freed from such liability. Finally, the right of a private individual to cause the drains of his premises to be connected with the water authority's sewerage system can be exercised only in relation to a public sewer.[3]

This problem of ownership really falls to be considered under two main headings, namely, the circumstances in which a sewer vests in the water authority (such a sewer is known[4] and hereafter described as a

---

[1] See post, Chap. 5, p. 64.
[2] Such as, e.g., s. 22 of the 1936 Act, enabling a water authority to alter the size or course of a sewer, or to discontinue or prohibit its use, either entirely, or for certain specified purposes; and see post, p. 80.
[3] See post, Chap. 9, p. 117.
[4] Act of 1936, s. 20 (2) (as amended). However, a sewer constructed by the water authority or their predecessor and vested in them did not before 1974 necessarily become a public sewer, if it was constructed after 1st October, 1937, solely for the purpose of draining property belonging to them, by virtue of s. 20 (2) in its original form, but this exception has now disappeared.

"public sewer"), and also the principles according to which the ownership of private sewers is to be determined.

2. PUBLIC SEWERS.

On a first perusal of section 20 of the 1936 Act (as re-enacted in Schedule 8 of the Water Act 1973), it would seem that the term "public sewer" is capable of easy comprehension and precise definition, being any sewer which is vested in the water authority by virtue of the section. The three classes of circumstances outlined in the section, in which a sewer becomes a public sewer, are, however, particularly difficult to apply, mainly because the law in force prior to the 1936 and 1973 Acts is in at least two respects incorporated by reference. These classifications must be dealt with *seriatim*. Thus, the Act of 1973 provides that the following are public sewers:

(a) **All sewers and disposal works constructed by the water authority** at their expense, or vested in the authority in pursuance of arrangements under section 15 of the Water Act 1973, or otherwise acquired by the authority.

So far as concerns sewers constructed on or after 1st April 1974 (when the Act of 1973 came into force), this raises no problems. If no arrangements are made under s. 15, such sewers vested in the district or London borough council (as successor to the county borough, borough, urban district or rural district council) on 1st April 1974, will remain so vested. But in the majority of cases such arrangements will be made and s. 15 gives compulsory powers to the Secretary of State where no arrangements are made by agreement. Whether or not arrangements are made sewers vested prior to 1.4.74 in the local authority will vest in the water authority (Act of 1973, s. 14 (2)) and to save complications it is presumed in this work that all public sewers vest in the water authority. We then have to face the further problem, what sewers vested in the local authority on 1st April 1974, and were so vested in its predecessor? The transfer from former local authority to new local authority on 1st April 1974 was of course effected by the Local Government Act 1972; see s. 181 (2).[1] The sewers that were then vested in the local authority were defined by section 20 of the 1936 Act in its original form, which then had *five* classifications of sewer for the purpose. Two of these were to all intents and purposes identical with sub-paras. *(b)* and *(c)* of section 20 (1) in its present form, discussed below, but the other three are as mentioned below, and therefore all sewers coming within any of these provisions are still public sewers. The three paragraphs of s. 20 (1) in its original form are:

> **(i) Sewers within the meaning of the Act of 1875**, which, by virtue of the provisions of that Act, were, immediately prior to the 1st October, 1937,[2] vested in the local authority.

In order to appreciate the effect of this provision, it is necessary to consider the relevant provisions of the Act of 1875, and the effect of the considerable case law arising therefrom, and the meaning of "sewer", as explained in Chap. 1, also must be borne in mind.

(i) *Meaning of "Sewer" in 1875 Act.*

The word "sewer" was defined by section 4 of the 1875 Act, to include "sewers and drains of every description, except drains to which the word 'drain' interpreted as aforesaid applies, and except drains vested in or under the control of any authority having the management of roads and not being a local authority under this Act"; "drain" in turn was defined in the

---

[1] Or in consequence of orders made under s. 254 or s. 68 of the 1972 Act.
[2] The date of the commencement of the 1936 Act; see s. 347 (1).

same section to mean[1] "any drain of and used for the drainage of one building only, or premises within the same curtilage, and made merely for the purpose of communicating therefrom with a cesspool or other like receptacle for drainage, or with a sewer into which the drainage of two or more buildings or premises occupied by different persons is conveyed." Speaking generally, therefore, by virtue of these definitions, a sewer was, for the purposes of the 1875 Act, any drain (or "line of pipes," to use a neutral expression), which served more than one building, or premises not within the same curtilage.[2] Even by reducing the provisions to this comparatively simple proposition one does not, however, explain the position fully, for the courts have had to consider the meanings in this connection of the term "building," and of the expression "within the same curtilage."

"Building" and "house" are not here necessarily synonymous, and it has been held to be a question of fact whether two semi-detached houses are a single building,[3] and the court, in a later case,[4] refused to lay down any general rule on the point. "Curtilage" is a legal term of ancient vintage, but none the less does not seem to be capable of precise definition; in the

---

[1] *Not* "include", as in the definition of "sewer". Strictly, a definition introduced by the word "includes" is not a definition at all; it leaves the word explained with its "ordinary" or dictionary meaning and adds to that meaning other terms not ordinarily included in the dictionary meaning. "Means", however, has an exclusionary effect—the definition is to be substituted for the word or words in the statute.

[2] Whether or not the sewer was laid in private land, if it were so laid, there would be no right to connect thereto without the consent of the landowner.

[3] Two such houses were held to be a single building for this purpose in *Hedley v. Webb*, [1901] 2 Ch. 126, but the converse had been held for the purpose of the Lands Clauses Consolidation Act, 1845, on slightly different facts, in *Harvie v. South Devon Railway Co.* (1874), 32 L.T. 1.

[4] *Humphrey v. Young*, [1903] 1 K.B. 44. In *Birch v. Wigan Corporation*, [1952] 2 All E.R. 893, a single house was held not to be capable of being part of a building for the purposes of the closing order provisions of the Housing Act, 1936 (*see* now s. 18 of the Housing Act, 1957) but this would not necessarily apply in the present context.

leading case of *Harris v. Scurfield*,[1] it was said,[2] "there is no definition of a curtilage which would include the case of a number of houses separately occupied by different people, simply because there is a common access and to some extent common accommodation." In one case,[3] two blocks of buildings belonging to the same owner and containing forty-six sets of apartments, were separated by a passageway some 20 feet wide, one end of which was open to a public highway. On the particular facts of the method of construction of these buildings, the court held that the two blocks were premises within the same curtilage. On the other hand, an arcade with a number of houses and shops on either side, and roofed over, with gates at either end, was held not to be buildings or premises within the same curtilage for the present purposes.[4]

The whole question of the meaning of drain for the purposes of the 1875 Act was re-considered by the House of Lords in *Weaver v Family Housing Association (York) Ltd.*[5] Their Lordships in considering whether a row of 8 houses could be regarded as one building, said that all the following matters were relevant, although they were not all to be given equal weight:

structural unity;
unit of ownership;
occupation by separate
    tenants, without
    intercommunication;

existence of a single
    comprehensive system
    of drainage;
separate cold stores;
separate outside
    lavatories.

Whilst refusing to interfere with the finding of the

---

[1] (1904), 68 J.P. 516.
[2] *Per* Alverstone, L.C.J.
[3] *Pilbrow v. St. Leonard's Shoreditch Vestry*, [1895] 1 Q.B. 433.
[4] *St. Martin's-in-the-Fields Vestry v. Bird*, [1895] 1 Q.B. 428.
[5] (1975) 74 L.G.R. 255.

Court below that these were separate buildings, their Lordships said that it was essentially a question of fact.

The Chancery Division (*per* Walton J) recently had a similar case before it.[1] The learned judge applied the cases discussed above including *Weaver*, and found that two separately occupied cottages built onto one another owned by the same landlord, were a single building, and that the water closets in the garden serving the cottages was within the curtilage of the building. Curtilage said his Lordship, was an "enclosure", or "land within an enclosure."

The essential point under this heading, therefore, is that the particular conduit (in order to be a public sewer) should drain two or more buildings.[2] The connection of a second building to an existing drain serving one building only, although done illegally and without the consent of the local authority, was nevertheless capable of operating to convert the drain into a public sewer as from the point of junction.[3] On the other hand, if one of the two premises drained by a public sewer is subsequently disconnected therefrom, such an action would not normally operate so as to make the sewer once more a drain.[4]

---

[1] *Cook v. Minion* [1979] J.P.L. 305.

[2] *Travis v. Uttley* [1894] 1 Q.B. 233; *Holland v. Lazarus* (1897) 66 L.J.Q.B. 285.

[3] *St. Matthew, Bethnal Green, Vestry v. London School Board*, [1898] A.C. 190, and compare *Holland v. Lazarus* (1897), 66 L.J.Q.B. 285. Both these decisions were on the provisions of the Metropolis Management Acts, but there seems to be no reason why the principle therein applied should not apply also to cases under the Public Health Acts.

[4] *St. Leonard, Shoreditch, Vestry v. Phelan* [1896] 1 Q.B. 533; but *see also Kershaw v. Smith*, [1913] 2 K.B. 455, in which Avory, J., refused to agree with the principle "once a sewer always a sewer," and held that a sewer which by reconstruction had become a drain serving but one building, could be no longer vested in the local authority as a public sewer. Where there was no such reconstruction, however, it was held that a sewer did not cease to be a sewer for the purposes of the 1936 Act just because it was not used as such: *Blackdown Properties Ltd. v. Minister of Housing and Local Government* [1965] 2 All E.R. 345. "Vesting" does not mean complete ownership, but merely the giving of an interest sufficient to enable the local authority to perform their duties; if those duties cease by a change in the factual situation then the vesting comes to an end; *see also Bradford v. Eastbourne Corporation*, [1896] 2 Q.B. 205, and article by the present writer at 20 Conv. N.S. 208.

Moreover, because a particular line of pipes served a number of premises, it did not necessarily follow that that conduit must be a public sewer from end to end.[1] That portion of the conduit which received the drainage of one building only would be a drain,[2] while the remainder could be a public sewer. If the conduit had been constructed by the local authority, or by a private individual with the approval of the local authority,[3] with the intention of it receiving the drainage of more than one building, it would normally be a public sewer, although no buildings might have been actually connected thereto.[4]

(ii) *"Vesting" under 1875 Act.*

Having decided that the particular line of pipes in question was a "sewer" within section 4 of the Act of 1875, it is then necessary to consider the effect of section 13 of that Act (now repealed), which reads as follows:

> "All existing and future sewers within the district of a local authority, together with all buildings, works, materials and things belonging thereto,[5] except—
>
>   (1) Sewers made by any person for his own profit, or by any company for the profit of the shareholders; and
>
>   (2) Sewers made and used[6] for the purpose of draining, preserving, or improving land under any local or private Act of Parliament, or for the purpose of irrigating land; and
>
>   (3) Sewers under the authority of any commis-

---

[1] As was suggested in *Travis v. Uttley (supra).*
[2] *Beckenham U.D.C. v. Wood* (1896), 60 J.P. 490.
[3] *Turner v. Handsworth U.D.C.,* [1909] 1 Ch. 381.
[4] *Turner v. Handsworth U.D.C.,* and *Beckenham U.D.C. v. Wood.*
[5] The position of sewage works, etc., is discussed *post,* Chap. 7, p. 102.
[6] The test here is probably the *primary* use for which the sewer in question was made. Difficulties may arise in practice where a land drain is also used for the conveyance of sewage.

sioners of sewers appointed by the Crown[1];
shall vest in and be under the control of
such local authority:

Provided that sewers within the district
of a local authority which have been or
which may hereafter be constructed by or
transferred to some other local authority or
by or to a sewage board or other authority
empowered under any Act of Parliament to
construct sewers shall (subject to any agreement to the contrary) vest in and be under
the control of the authority who constructed
the same, or to whom the same have been
transferred."

The second and third[2] exceptions from the general
proposition in this section are virtually self-
explanatory,[3] and do not normally give rise to difficulties, but the exception of sewers made "by any person
for his own profit," has been the subject of considerable judicial interpretation. Whether or not a particular
sewer was made for profit is essentially a question of
fact.[4] Thus, a sewer constructed by a builder laying out
a building estate is still capable of not having been

---

[1] *Ante*, p. 1.

[2] The second exception clearly deals with land drainage; the third deals
with sewers that are not normally the concern of the local authority as such
(except with the consent of the appropriate Government Department under,
e.g., s. 327 of the Act of 1875). The proviso to the section does not cause
difficulty, this relating to public sewers constructed by a public body for
public use.

[3] It is largely a question of fact and degree as to whether a land drain has
become a sewer. If the ditch takes a considerable amount of surface water
from houses, this may make it a sewer: *Ferrand v. Hellas Land & Building
Co.*, [1893] 2 Q.B. 135; but *see R. v. Godmanchester L.B.* (1866), L.R. 1
Q.B. 328.

[4] *Southstrand Estate Development Co. v. East Preston R.D.C.*, [1934]
Ch. 254; unfortunately, it is only too often in this branch of the law that
one finds that a particular matter is to be treated by the courts as a "question
of fact". The result is, that every such problem must be considered in
relation to all the relevant circumstances, and reference to previously decided cases, except perhaps to indicate *which* circumstances are likely to be
considered relevant, is not of any great assistance.

made for profit, although the builder proposes to sell off the houses, when constructed, and makes a profit out of the transaction.[1] On the other hand, "profit" in the section does not necessarily mean a direct money payment, and a land drain constructed for the purpose of enabling the land to be used more economically would normally be held to be one made for profit.[2]

To summarise the effect, therefore, of this first class of sewers vested in the local authority under section 20 of the 1936 Act in its original form, it seems that every "line of pipes" which was a "sewer" and was constructed prior to 1st October, 1937, for the drainage of more than one building, or for premises not within the same curtilage, and which was not made for profit, vested in the former local authority under the 1875 Act, and will now normally be vested in the water authority under s. 20 of the 1936 Act in its new form.[3] It is also clear that a sewer constructed mainly for the purpose of taking surface water from buildings is none the less capable of being a public sewer, although it may also take land drainage.[4]

(ii) All combined drains constructed before the 1st October, 1937,[5] which, by virtue of the Act of 1875 would, immediately before the 1st October, 1937,[4] have been vested in the local authority as sewers

---

[1] *Ferrand v. Hallas Land & Building Co.,* [1893] 2 Q.B. 135; *Pinnock v. Waterworth* (1887), 3 T.L.R. 563; the fact that the builder intends to reimburse himself for his expenses in constructing the sewer does not affect the position; *Vowles v. Colmer* (1895), 64 L.J. Ch. 414, which was followed in *Solihull R.D.C. v. Ford* (1932), 30 L.G.R. 483. "Made for profit" is not the same thing as "made for use," said Huddleston, B., in *Bonella v. Twickenham Local Board* (1887), 18 Q.B.D. 577.
[2] *Croysdale v. Sunbury-on-Thames U.D.C.,* [1898] 2 Ch. 515. A sewer constructed for the purpose of draining agricultural land will also normally be held to have been one made for profit and hence not a sewer within the section: *Phillimore v. Watford R.D.C.,* [1913] 2 Ch. 434, and *see Vare v. Joy* (1920), 124 L.T. 148.
[3] Subject to the possible exception of "single private drains", considered under class **(ii)**, below.
[4] *Hutton v. Esher U.D.C.* [1973] 2 All E.R. 1123.
[5] The date of commencement of the 1936 Act: *see* s. 347 (1).

but for the provisions of some enactment or statutory scheme relating to the construction of combined drains, or of an order made under such an enactment or scheme.

This provision also needs a consideration of the pre-1936 Act law for its appreciation. It will be noted in the first place that the paragraph applies only to "combined drains". This expression was not defined in the 1875 Act, nor is a definition included in the 1936 Act; it must therefore be construed as a technical term, referring to the common practice of builders and others engaged in the construction of drains. Generally speaking, buildings may be said to be drained in combination where a common line of pipes taken the effluent from the internal drains of the several buildings through private land to a cesspool, cesspit or "other receptacle for drainage," or to a sewer. By reason of the definitions of "sewer" and "drain" in section 4 of the Act of 1875,[1] every combined drain having a proper outfall[1] was itself a sewer and under section 13 of the same Act, vested in the local authority. The present paragraph does not, therefore, seem strictly to be necessary, as every such combined drain/public sewer will already remain vested in the local authority under class (i), discussed above (p. 12).

"Vesting" in the local authority under section 13 of the 1875 Act, did not, however, give the authority an absolute right of ownership in the sewer in question,[2] as the section did not make the sewers the property of the authority so as to place them to all intents and purposes in the same position as if they were the private owners of the sewers. Thus the authority have no power to stop up a sewer vested in them, or physically to

---

[1] *Supra*, p. 12.
[2] *Attorney-General v. Dorking Union* (1882), 20 Ch. D. 595: "We must remember that the vesting of the sewers in the local authority gives them a very limited right of ownership": *per* Jessel, M.R., at p. 604.

disconnect drains therefrom.[1] This limitation on the effect of the statutory vesting was important after the passing of the Public Health Acts Amendment Act, 1890,[2] section 19 of which read as follows:

"(1) Where two or more houses belonging to different owners are connected with a public sewer by a single private drain, an application may be made under section 41 of the Act of 1875[3] (relating to complaints as to nuisances from drains), and the local authority may recover any expenses incurred by them in executing any works under the powers conferred on them by that section from the owners of the houses in such shares and proportions as shall be settled by their surveyor or (in case of dispute) by a court of summary jurisdiction.

(2) Such expenses may be recovered summarily or may be declared by the urban authority to be private improvement expenses under the Public Health Acts, and may be recovered accordingly.

(3) For the purposes of this section the expres-

---

[1] *Ogilvie v. Blything Union Rural Sanitary Authority* (1891), 65 L.T. 338; (1892), 67 L.T. 18. "It has been clearly held that the vesting is not a giving of the property of the sewer and in the soil surrounding it to the local authority, but gives such ownership and such rights only as are necessary for the purpose of carrying out the duties of a local authority with regard to the subject matter"; *per* Lord Russell, C. J., in *Bradford v. Mayor of Eastbourne*, [1896] 2 Q.B. 205. In *Newcastle Corporation v. Woolstanton Ltd.*, [1947] 1 All E.R. 218, it was held that a gas undertaking has no natural right of support (apart from statute) for the land surrounding its gas mains, but only an implied right of support for the mains themselves (and *see* Chap. 5, *post*, p. 87); it seems that this principle applies equally to public sewers. *See* now s. 22 of the 1936 Act, *post*, p. 80.
[2] And provided the section had been adopted by the local authority concerned, this being an adoptive Act; the section was repealed by the 1936 Act.
[3] Under this section the local authority, on complaint made to them of a nuisance in a drain, privy, cesspool, etc., could take certain action to secure the abatement of the nuisance, and if necessary take default action, their expenses in so doing being recoverable from the owner of the premises concerned.

sion 'drain' includes a drain used for the drainage of more than one building."

The term "single private drain" in this section was not given a statutory definition, but it received much judicial consideration. The section is considered further later[1]; suffice it here to summarise the cases by describing the expression as a drainage pipe provided for a single house or for a group of houses in common, which is exclusive and private to that house or those houses.[2] Many of these drains which serve more than one house will also be combined drains, and if constructed before 1st October, 1937, would therefore have vested in the local authority under the present paragraph; unless the two or more houses served by a particular drain were one building, or premises within the same curtilage.[3] It is submitted that the present paragraph in so far as it relates to section 19 of the 1890 Act was included in the 1936 Act *ex abundanti cautela*, and so as to answer the argument that the 1890 Act at least in part divested the property in a sewer previously vested under the 1875 Act; it was argued (wrongly as it seems) for instance,[4] that a single private drain could not also be a public sewer.[5]

A similar position would appear to arise in connection with the common form provision in many local Acts,[6] in force before the passing of the 1936 Act, by

---

[1] *See* Chap. 5, *post*, p. 73.
[2] *Kingston-upon-Hull Corporation v. North-Eastern Railway Co.*, [1916] 1 Ch. 31; the houses must be in separate ownership for s. 19 of the 1890 Act to apply.
[3] *See* definitions of "sewer" and "drain" in s. 4 of the 1875 Act: *supra*, p. 12.
[4] *E.g.* in *Hill v. Aldershot Corporation*, [1933] 1 K.B. 259, and *post*, p. 74.
[5] In *Pemsel and Wilson v. Tucker*, [1907] 2 Ch. 191, a "single private drain" within the meaning of s. 19 of the Act of 1890 was held none the less to have vested in the local authority as a sewer; the 1890 Act did not operate to prevent this vesting, and the owner of the property concerned therefore could not convey to a purchaser the property in the sewer.
[6] "Enactment" includes any enactment in a provisional order confirmed by Parliament: s. 343 (1) of the 1936 Act.

which the effect of the section of the 1890 Act above discussed was made applicable to a "single private drain" serving two or more houses owned by the same person, or by different persons.[1] Such a provision also would not, it is submitted, have affected the vesting of the sewer under the Act of 1875.[2]

The present paragraph in the 1936 Act also referred to "statutory schemes",[3] the commonest examples of which in practice were the planning schemes prepared under the Town and Country Planning Act, 1932, and its predecessors. Such schemes frequently made provision for the combined drainage of houses[4]; this paragraph will cover any combined drain constructed under such a scheme before the 1st October, 1937.

Other local Acts may contain different provisions which would be affected by this paragraph[5]; these ob-

---

[1] *See, e.g.*, s. 49 of the Kingston-upon-Hull Corporation Act, 1903, considered by the Court in *Kingston-upon-Hull v. North-Eastern Railway Co.*, *supra*.

[2] *Ibid.*

[3] Defined by s. 343 (1) of the 1936 Act as meaning schemes "made under any enactment".

[4] A combined drainage agreement is valid and enforceable by the local authority (*Butt v. Snow* (1903), 67 J.P. 454) with whom it is made, but only against the original owner, as the stipulations in the agreement will be positive in character and would not, therefore, run with the land as would restrictive covenants (*see, e.g. Haywood v. Brunswick Building Society* (1882), 8 Q.B.D. 403). By incorporating such agreements in the local authority's planning scheme under the Town and Country Planning Act 1932, this difficulty of enforceability was overcome. The agreements made under such a scheme frequently provided that the financial responsibility of maintaining the drains in question would remain with the private owners concerned.

[5] Under the Metropolis Management Acts, the term "drain" was defined to include "any drain for draining any group or block of houses by a combined operation under the order of any vestry" (*see* s. 250 of the Metropolis Management Act, 1855). The Public Health Acts apply to central London only with modifications; cases decided on the statutes relating to London shold therefore be read and applied with caution and reserve. A number of local Acts provided that the local authority should be enabled to order the provision of combined drainage; such cases, outside the Metropolis, might have operated prior to the 1936 Act, to prevent such combined drains from vesting in the local authority (*see, e.g.*, s. 81 of the Wimbledon Corporation Act, 1914, discussed in *Grant. v. Derwent*, [1929] 1 Ch. 390).

viously cannot be dealt with in detail in the present context.

Before temporarily leaving the subject of combined drains, it should, perhaps, be mentioned that the term is not here used in the sense sometimes used by engineers and other technicians, namely, to indicate that the particular drain is used for the conveyance of both foul and surface water.

> **(iii) All sewers constructed by the local authority at their expense or acquired by them:** provided that a sewer constructed by the authority after the 1st October, 1937,[1] for the purpose only of draining property belonging to them, is not to be deemed to be a public sewer under the 1936 Act, until it has been declared to be a public sewer.[2]

It will be observed that this class of public sewer refers only to sewers properly so-called,[3] but includes sewers constructed either prior or subsequent to the commencement of the 1936 Act. Moreover, it would include a sewer constructed by the predecessors in title of the local authority, either as landowner or as sanitary authority, by virtue of the reference to "acquisition".

The sewer need not have been constructed by the local authority in its capacity of local sanitary authority; it may, for example, have been constructed for the purpose of draining the authority's housing estate, under the Housing Act, 1957; in such a case, the proviso would normally apply, and the sewer did not become a public one until the authority had declared it to be such. No particular formality had to be observed in the making of such a declaration; an ordinary resolution of the authority was probably sufficient. This provision applied also to sewers constructed by a local authority

---

[1] The commencement of the 1936 Act: see s. 347 (1).
[2] Act of 1936, s. 20 (2) proviso.
[3] See Chap. 1, ante, p. 1, et seq.

outside their own district, under sections 15 and 16 of the 1936 Act.[1]

The proviso does not appear in the existing version of section 20, but in view of the terms of s. 20 (1) (*a*) this is immaterial as the paragraph refers to sewers constructed by the water authority not by the local authority. There is therefore no question of a sewer constructed by the local authority after 1.4.74 becoming a public sewer, unless and until it is "adopted" by the water authority or arrangements are made under s. 15 of the 1973 Act.

A sewer constructed by the local authority, but at the expense of some other person[2] did not vest in the authority under this provision, and (if constructed after the commencement of the Act) remains a private sewer.

The remainder of the section 20(1) in its new form provides for the vesting of the following:—

> **(b) All sewers constructed under Part IX of the Highways Act, 1959,** [see now Part XI of the Highways Act 1980] except sewers belonging to a road maintained by the highway authority.

This paragraph refers to the procedure for the making up of private streets at the expense, partial or complete, of the frontagers, under Part XI of the Highways Act, 1980.[3] These provisions enable the highway authority[4] to require a private street to be sewered, levelled, paved, metalled, flagged, channelled, made

---

[1] Now repealed: *see post*, Chapter 3, p. 35.
[2] *E.g.*, under s. 36 of the 1936 Act (*see* s. 36 (3)); or by agreement with the owner or occupier of the premises concerned, under s. 275. *ibid.*
[3] There is now only one such procedure, that under "the code of 1892"; the former procedure by way of "the code of 1875" was abolished by the Local Government Act 1972.
[4] The county council or the London Borough council.

good[1] or lighted to the satisfaction of the authority; any
one or more of these operations can be required to be
executed at the same time. Once a sewer has been
constructed under either of these provisions, it becomes a public sewer and vests in the water authority,
and where the authority had expressed themselves as
satisfied with a particular system of sewering, they
could not require the owners of the private street in
question to construct a further sewer, should this subsequently become necessary.[2] It does not, however,
necessarily follow that, because a particular sewer laid
in a private street is vested in the water authority as a
public sewer under some paragraph other than that
under discussion, that such street is sewered to the
"satisfaction" of the authority, so as to prevent the
authority from taking any further action under the private street works legislation in respect thereof.[3]

Highway drains vest in the highway authority,[4] and
consequently the exception in the present paragraph
provides that where the private street works action is
confined to the construction of a highway drain or
sewer, any sewer so constructed will vest in the highway
authority and will not be a "public sewer".

(c) All sewers and sewage disposal works with re-spect to which a declaration of vesting made under the 1936 Act (as amended)[5] has taken effect.

This paragraph is fully discussed *post*, Chap. 4, p. 57,
et. seq.

In addition a public sewer may vest in the water authority under a transitional agreement made under s.

---

[1] This particular operation did not appear in the code of 1875; otherwise
the two codes were similar.
[2] *Bonella v. Twickenham Local Board* (1888), 20 Q.B.D. 63; *Poole Corporation v. Blake*, [1955] 3 All E.R. 409.
[3] It is a question of fact in each case whether or not the local authority
were so satisfied; *post*, Chap. 6, p. 98.
[4] *See post*, Chap. 6, p. 91.
[5] Under Part II thereof.

68 of the Local Government Act 1972, or by an order made by the Secretary of State under section 254, *ibid.*

Conclusion.

To close this summary of the legal definition of the term "public sewer," it should be added that every sewer that is not a public sewer by virtue of one or more of the three headings of section 20 in its amended form (incorporating the three limbs of the original form of the section, as explained), is a private sewer, and will be vested not in the water or local authority, but in some private individual. Every public sewer (but highway drains in highways may seem to be an exception[1]), is vested in the water authority.

3. THE EFFECT OF PUBLIC OWNERSHIP.

If a particular conduit is in law a public sewer, it will normally be vested in the water authority, but their ownership thereof will be limited, as above explained[2] to the purposes of fulfilling their functions as sewerage authority. Further, they will not be able to interfere with private rights enjoyed in respect of the particular conduit before it became a public sewer,[3] nor may they physically disconnect any drains from the public sewer (except under section 42 of the 1936 Act).[4] However, the following consequences will apply in the event of a conduit being in law a public sewer:

> (*a*) the water authority will be under a duty to maintain, cleanse and empty it[5];
>
> (*b*) provided he has a means of access thereto an

---

[1] Trunk and special roads are vested in the Secretary of State under the Highways Act, 1980, and other highways vest in the county council. In Greater London, most highways vest in the London Borough council, but metropolitan roads vest in the Greater London Council.
[2] *Ante*, p. 15.
[3] *See, e. g., R. v. Staines Local Board* (1888), 60 L.T. 261.
[4] *Ogilvie v. Blything Union R.S.A.* (1891), 65 L.T. 338.
[5] 1936 Act, s. 23; *post*, p. 64.

adjoining landowner will have a right to cause the drains of his premises to connect thereto[1];

(c) the water authority will not be able to take proceedings (*e. g.*, in nuisance) in respect of any effluent therefrom (but *see* s. 55 of the 1974 Act).

(d) the **local** authority may be able to prevent building over the sewer[2] and the water authority will be able to take proceedings if anyone interferes with their property.[3]

Thus, for example, in the diagram on page 28, the drain although it serves more than one premises, is **not** a public sewer (whether constructed before or after 1st October, 1937); indeed it is not a sewer at all, as it does not lead to a proper outfall (*ante*, page 4). Therefore if flooding occurs at the shaded area the water authority would not themselves be liable, but the local authority could probably commence nuisance proceedings against the persons responsible, who will presumably be the owners of A, B and C. If there is a highway drain connected at point E, this will not affect the position, as the frontagers would be liable. However, if Lovers' Lane were adopted by the highway authority, and the flooding was shown to be due to the surface water from the highway, that authority would (presumably) be held liable.

Further if a new house is built on plot D, the owner will have no right to cause his house drains to connect with this existing drain; he would have to negotiate terms with the owners of A, B, and C.

---

[1] *Ibid*, s. 34, *post*, p. 118.
[2] *Ibid*, s. 25, *post*, p. 82.
[3] *Post*, p. 84.

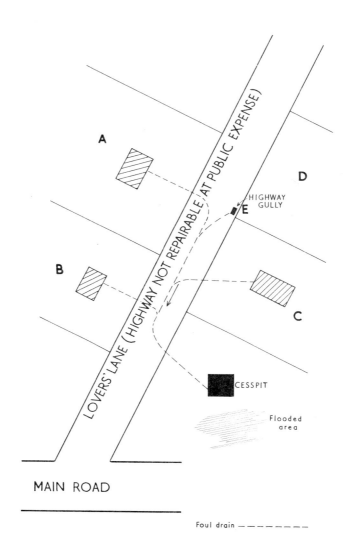

MAIN ROAD

Foul drain — — — — — — —

4. PRIVATE SEWERS.

A sewer which is not a public sewer must be a private sewer, and there is no point, in law, of distinguishing between a private sewer and a drain.[1] "Sewer" will normally be used to describe a conduit draining more than one property, and "drain" will be used to signify a channel draining a single property,[2] but the distinction has no legal significance. The all important question is, whether a particular sewer is a **public** sewer.

In practice, however, the subsidiary question may arise, in whom is a particular private sewer or drain vested? If the sewer drains the premises and runs through the land of but a single owner, it is normally clear that such owner is the owner of the sewer; if the sewer is used to drain the property of another person, the legal position (in the absence of any express agreement or provision in the relevant title deeds) will be presumed to be that the owner of the tenement has granted an easement of drainage through his property—provided the requirements for presuming such an easement are present. Thus (apart from an express grant), the right must have continued for the statutory period for prescription of 20 years,[3] the dominant owner must have enjoyed the easement claimed as a benefit for his property of which he is owner in fee simple, the

---

[1] A drain, *stricto sensu*, cannot be vested in the water authority as sanitary authority, although it may, of course, belong to the authority or to the local authority in their capacity as landowners, or by virtue of its draining the authority's own property. *See also* definition of "private sewer" in s. 343 (1) of the 1936 Act.

[2] Buildings drained "in combination" are, however, said to be served by a combined "drain".

[3] Prescription Act, 1832. User for 20 years may be defeated by evidence proving that no easement had in fact been granted (for all prescription depends on a presumed grant), but user for 40 years is indefeasible, except by proof that the user had originally been by agreement or consent (*see* s. 2 of the Act of 1832). A right to cause sewage to flow across another's land or into a public sewer cannot be acquired secretly without the knowledge of the owner of the servient tenement: *Liverpool Corporation v. Coghill*, [1918] 1 Ch. 307.

use of the sewer must be claimed "as of right",[1] and the right claimed must be to drain through a well defined channel.[2]

It is frequently important to decide whether a particular person has an easement to lay a private sewer or drain through another person's land,[3] for if the conduit is there with the permission of the landowner in such circumstances that an easement has been created, that landowner will not be able to require the removal of the conduit without making payment of compensation to the person entitled to use the drain.[4] However,

[1] The user must therefore have commenced "*nec vi nec clam nec precario,*", *i.e.*, permission must not have been obtained by force, or the user must not have commenced secretly and in such circumstances that the owner of the servient tenement could not have been aware of the drain in question, or with the permission of the owner of the servient tenement, as in such last-mentioned case, the right would be limited to the terms of such permission. On these points, *see* such cases as *Union Lighterage Co. v. London Graving Dock Co.*, [1902] 2 Ch. 557, and *Lyell v. Hothfield*, [1914] 3 K.B. 911.

[2] This proposition follows, it is submitted, from the law relating to the acquisition of rights to watercourses; thus, in *Acton v. Blundell* (1843), 12 M. & W. 324, it was held that a landowner could have no rights in water percolating in an undefined channel through his land in such manner as to enable him to prevent an adjoining owner from diverting such water.

[3] The right to lay a drain and to cause drainage to flow through such drain will normally carry with it the ancillary rights to enter on the land and effect necessary works of repair, maintenance or renewal to the drain; see *Pomfret v. Ricroft* (1669), 1 Saund. 321. It would not, of course, since such a right be competent to increase the size of the drain. In *Sunmons v. Midford* [1969] 2 All E.R. 1269, it was held, on the facts of that case, that a grant of an easement of drainage amounted to an exclusive right to use the line of pipes in question.

[4] An easement is a legal interest provided it is created by grant (express, implied or presumed from long use) and limited for an interest equivalent to an estate in fee simple absolute in possession or a term of years absolute: Law of Property Act, 1925, s. 1 (2) *(a)*. If the easement of drainage in question is a legal interest, it will be enforceable against subsequent purchasers of the servient tenement. If it has been limited in such a manner that it is capable of subsisting only as an equitable interest in the land, it will none the less still be enforceable against subsequent owners, provided it is registered as an equitable easement under s. 2 (5) of the Land Charges Act 1972 (Class D (iii)). Easements granted for drains to serve an estate to be developed subsequent to the time of the grant should be limited so as to take effect within the perpetuity period: *Dunn v. Blackdown Properties Ltd.* [1961] 2 All E.R. 62. However, in the case of deeds coming into effect after 1964, an easement which is in fact exercised within the perpetuity period will not be invalidated simply because it could have first been exercised after the end of that period; one is now entitled to "wait and see" if there will be a breach of the perpetuity rule: Perpetuities and Accumulations Act, 1964, s. 3.

when taking proceedings for the abatement of a nuisance[1] in a private sewer or drain, or caused thereby, the local authority are not concerned to ascertain whether the persons whose premises are drained by the conduit in question have a legal right to cause their drainage to flow through such conduit[2]; they will be the persons by "whose act, default, or sufferance"[3] the nuisance has arisen or is continuing, and abatement proceedings may, therefore, properly be taken against them.[4] On the other hand, the landowner who stops up a private sewer laid through his land without his consent may be liable in nuisance abatement proceedings brought by the local authority, as he would then be the person who had caused the nuisance.[5] The owner of a private sewer or drain may be liable in private nuisance to another landowner who has sustained injury as a consequence of his failure to cleanse the sewer, etc.[6]

---

[1] Under the "nuisance clauses" (ss. 92–100) or s. 39 of the 1936 Act,

[2] *Brown v. Bussell* (1868), L.R., 3 Q.B. 251.

[3] *See* s. 93 of the 1936 Act.

[4] If the drain is really a public sewer vested in the water authority, apparently no nuisance proceedings can be taken against a person draining into it, and in respect of whom it might otherwise be said that he was causing a nuisance: *Fordom v. Parsons*, [1894] 2 Q.B. 780. The judgment of Kennedy, J., in *Wincanton R.D.C. v. Parsons*, [1905] 2 K.B. 34, however, suggests that the fact that the conduit in question was a public sewer, would not necessarily constitute a defence in nuisance proceedings. It is submitted that this decision, in so far as this point is concerned, would not be followed (*see* Lumley's Public Health, 12th edn., Vol. III, p. 2278).

[5] *Riddell v. Spear* (1879), 43 J.P. 317; but it should be noted that in this case the sewer in question had become a public sewer before the action complained of was taken.

[6] *Sedleigh-Denfield v. O'Callaghan* [1940] 3 All E.R. 349.

CHAPTER 3

CONSTRUCTION OF PUBLIC SEWERS

1. INTRODUCTORY.

Under section 14 of the Water Act 1973, it is made the express duty of each water authority "to provide either inside or outside their area such public sewers as may be necessary for effectually draining their area". Section 14 replaces section 14 of the Public Health Act 1936 imposing a similar duty on the local authority, and this section itself replaced the effect, in part,[1] of section 15 of the 1875 Act, in which statute it was provided[2] that, where a local authority had made default in providing their district with sufficient sewers or in the maintenance of existing sewers, a complaint could be made to the Local Government Board,[3] who could then make a default order, compelling the authority to carry out their statutory duties in that respect. The power to make a complaint and the consequential default powers of the Secretary of State are now contained in section 322 of the 1936 Act which in this respect would seem not to apply to water authorities.[4]

---

[1] Section 15 of the 1875 Act, unlike its opposite number in the 1936 Act, also provided for the maintenance by the local authority of existing sewers. This is covered in the 1936 Act, by s. 23 thereof (see Chap. 5, post, p. 64).

[2] By s. 299 thereof; both this section and s. 15 of the 1875 Act have been repealed by the 1936 Act.

[3] The duties of the Board are now vested in the Secretary of State for the Environment, Chap. 1, ante, p. 8.

[4] Section 14 of the 1936 Act, relating to the duty to provide a sewer under that Act, has been repealed and is therefore not included in the sections transferred to water authorities and consequently it seems that the default powers of the Secretary of State cannot be applied to the duties of water authorities under s. 14 of the Act of 1973.

It was held on several occasions in the Courts that the joint effect of the two provisions in the 1875 Act was to exclude the jurisdiction of the Courts in these matters. As the legislature had provided a specific remedy, they must be presumed to have excluded any alternative remedy, and therefore under the pre-1974 law no action for damages would lie against a local authority, based on their default in failing to provide a public sewer.[1] The water authority would be in the same position in relation to any pre-1974 default of a predecessor local authority.

As the procedure by way of a complaint under section 322 is not available against a water authority in respect of section 14[2], it seems that proceedings for a *mandamus*, or in an appropriate case an action for damages, will lie against a defaulting water authority.

The duty under section 14 of the 1973 Act will, it should be noted, extend only to the provision of sewers and does not include the provision of land drains or drains required for agricultural purposes, as the duty

---

[1] This principle was based on the wording of the sections here discussed (*see. e.g., Robinson v. Corporation of Workington*, [1897] 1 Q.B. 619), and not, it is submitted, on an extension of the common law doctrine of immunity in respect of non-feasance, which formerly applied to highway authorities only, and only when acting as such (*see Cowley v. Newmarket Local Board*, [1892] A.C. 345, and *Skilton v. Epsom and Ewell U.D.C.*, [1936], 2 All E.R. 50). As a consequence of the proposition above stated, *mandamus* would not be granted to compel an authority to provide an adequate sewerage system (*Pasmore v. Oswaldtwistle U.D.C.*, [1898] A.C.387), nor could an action be brought to obtain a declaration to the effect that a particular conduit is repairable by the local authority (*Clark v. Epsom R. D.C.*, [1929] 1 Ch. 287). It is appreciated that these decisions were based on the wording of the 1875 Act, and that there has been no reported decision on the point since the passing of the 1936 Act, but it is submitted (*see* text, *infra*), that the general principle is also applicable to the sections of the 1936 Act. As is so often the case in this subject, in order to understand a statute expressed to "consolidate with amendments certain enactments relating to public health," recourse must be had to the law in force before the 1936 Act came on the statute book. The general principle that where a statute has provided a specific type of remedy for a particular grievance, that remedy alone is available to a person aggrieved, was again confirmed in *Cutler v. Wandsworth Stadium*, [1949] A.C. 398.
[2] *Aliter* with the duty under section 23 of the 1936 Act, see *post* page 64.

is to provide only **public** sewers, *i.e.*, sewers which will when constructed, vest in the authority as public sewers under section 20 of the 1936 Act as amended.

Under section 16 of the 1973 Act, it becomes the duty of a water authority to provide a public sewer, to be used for domestic purposes,[1] for the drainage of premises [one or more] in their area if the owners or occupiers of the premises to be served require them to do so. Conditions as to the charges in respect of the drainage of premises served by such a public sewer that will be recoverable, have to be satisfied before the water authority need meet such a requirement, and the water authority may require a landowner to deposit a sum as security for the payment of charges, but this deposit may not exceed the total expense of laying the sewer. Nothing in section 14 (the duty to provide a sewer) is to be read as overriding the requirements of this section (*see* subs. (14)).

Section 16 is an important provision, enabling a developer to ensure that the sewerage system will be extended to meet his needs; apart from this section a local authority had to reach an agreement with the developer, and they would normally require the total capital cost of any such new sewers to be borne by the developer in advance. The section is similar to the provision for water main extension in s. 37 of the Water Act, 1945, and is simpler in administration by reason of the system under the 1973 Act and the Water Charges Act 1976 for the financing of the sewage and sewerage functions of water authorities.[2]

---

[1] An expression which is defined for the purposes of this Act by s. 16 (12), and *see post*, p. 146.
[2] *Post*, p. 107.

2. RIGHTS TO LAY SEWERS.

A water authority which proposes to construct a new sewer[1] must first obtain the necessary rights to lay the pipes, manholes, etc., through and in the land in the selected positions. These rights may be obtained by agreement, or more commonly, compulsorily under the power given by section 15 of the 1936 Act (as amended). This section is speedy and simple to operate in practice, and also satisfactorily safeguards the interests of the landowner affected, and is therefore used by most authorities in prefereence to the negotiation of rights by agreement; moreover, if the procedure under the section is used, the authority may be assured that all the necessary ancillary rights (such as power of entry[2]) are exercisable in conjunction with the right itself.

Section 15 of the 1936 Act as amended by Schedule 8 of the Act of 1973, empowers a water authority to take the following action, when operating either inside or outside their area. These powers may also be conferred on a new town development corporation by an order made by the Secretary of State under section 34 of the New Towns Act 1965 (as amended by Sched. 8 of the Act of 1973).[3] No special procedure now has to be followed if the sewer is to be laid **outside** the area of the water authority concerned.

(i) *To construct a public sewer in, under or over any street, or under any cellar or vault below any street.*

---

[1] We are here using the term "sewer" to mean "public sewer," constructed by the water authority at their expense (*see* s. 20 (1) (*a*) of the 1936 Act, Chap. 2, *ante*, p. 11). The rules governing the construction of the private sewers of a local authority (*e.g.*, for draining their housing estates), are those provided for in the relevant enabling statute and are not, strictly speaking, part of the law of public health (the provision of a sewer for a housing estate would be regarded as an ancillary power, covered by s. 92 and s. 107 of the Housing Act, 1957).

[2] Under s. 287 of the 1936 Act: *see* Chap. 11, *post*, p. 176.

[3] And see *ante*, page 7.

In exercising this power, the water authority must observe the provisions of the Third Schedule to the Water Act, 1945 (Part VI), and the street works code contained in the Public Utilities Street Works Act, 1950, relating to the breaking-up of streets, as applied to the 1936 Act.[1] In practice the work may actually be undertaken by the district council acting as agents for the water authority pursuant to arrangements made under s. 15 (1) of the Water Act 1973.

When proposing to break up a street, the authority must give at least 14 clear days' notice before commencing the work, except in cases of emergency, to the persons having control of the street or bridge (in any case of a highway over a bridge),[2] they must be careful to cause as little damage as "may be",[3] execute the work in such a manner as to cause as little interference to traffic as possible (but the sewer may be laid *overground*),[4] and make compensation for any damage done as a consequence of breaking-up.[5] The water authority may execute works of breaking open a street, which amount to "code-regulated works", only after a plan and section thereof have been settled in accordance with the procedure contained in sections 3–5 of the Public Utilities Street Works Act, 1950. In the case of a private street,[6] the street managers and in the case of a trunk or special road the Secretary of State, will be concerned. In most circumstances notice must be given

---

[1] *See* s. 279 (1) of the 1936 Act, as amended by the Fourth Schedule to the Water Act, 1945, and the Act of 1950. The latter Act repeals s. 279 (2) and (3); ss. 280 and 281 of the 1936 Act had already been repealed by the Water Act, 1945.

[2] This will normally be the local highway authority, or in the case of a trunk or special road, the Secretary of State for the Environment. As to highways over bridges, *see* definition of "street" given in the text, below.

[3] Water Act, 1945, Third Schedule, para. 22.

[4] *Roderick v. Aston Local Board* (1877), 5 Ch. D. 328.

[5] Water Act, 1945, Third Schedule, para. 22, and 1936 Act, s. 278.

[6] Unless the private street has been declared to be a "prospectively maintainable highway", under the Second Schedule to the 1950 Act, in which case the highway authority will be concerned.

to the highway authority before the works are commenced.[1] It is further the responsibility of the authority constructing the sewer to cause the opening to be fenced and guarded, and adequately lit at night, and proper traffic signs to be placed and operated as may be required.[2] Interim reinstatement will normally be the responsibility of the undertaking authority, and the highway authority may elect to do the final reinstatement; if the sewer authority themselves (as "undertakers") do the final reinstatement, they may be liable for any subsidence occurring within six months.[3] In the event of any breach of the provisions of the 1950 Act or of the 1945 Act by the authority constructing the sewer, they may be liable to prosecution.[4] A street or bridge under the control of, or repairable by, the British Railways Board,[5] or any dock undertakers, may not ("except in cases of emergency arising from defects in pipes, plants or works") be opened or broken-up without their consent, but such consent may not be unreasonably withheld.[6] The powers given by section 290 of the Highways Act, 1980 (formerly section 153 of the 1875 Act)[7] to a local authority to require water or gas pipes, mains, plugs or other waterworks or gasworks laid in or under any street to be moved, apply for the purposes of the present section.[8]

Powers to close roads to traffic during the execution of sewerage works are exercisable by the highway authority by orders made under section 12 of the Road Traffic Regulation Act, 1967.

---

[1] 1950 Act, s. 6.
[2] *Ibid.*, s. 8.
[3] *Ibid.*, s. 7.
[4] Water Act, Third Schedule, para. 27 (1).
[5] Formerly the railway companies and then the Railway Executive, but *see* now Transport Act, 1962.
[6] Water Act, 1945, Third Schedule, para. 25, as amended by the Public Utilities Street Works Act, 1950.
[7] This section has not been repealed by the 1936 Act or the 1950 Act.
[8] 1936 Act, s. 282.

"Street" is defined for the purposes of the 1936 Act as including[1] "any highway, including a highway over any bridge, and any road, lane, footway, square, court, alley or passage, whether a thoroughfare or not".[2] For the purposes of the Third Schedule to the Water Act of 1945, the term also includes (see para. 28 thereof) "any land within the limits of a street but not included in the roadway or footpath thereof, as if that land were, or formed part of, a footpath of the street". The term is even more widely defined in the Public Utilities Street Works Act, 1950, as including "any length of land laid out as a way whether it is for the time being formed as a way or not".[3] A highway must be a way over which members of the public have a right to pass and re-pass on their lawful occasions, but it need not necessarily be maintainable at the public expense.

As stated above, in exercising this power to construct a sewer in, under or over a street, the authority must do so in a proper and reasonably careful manner; they will be liable in damages to any lawful user of the highway who suffers injury as a consequence of the subsidence of the highway, or otherwise, which is due to the negligent manner of construction of the sewer by the authority.[4] Any authority carrying out works on a public highway have a special duty of care owed towards any member of the public who may sustain injury as a consequence thereof.[5] Moreover, if the sewer[6] is not properly maintained, the water authority will be

---

[1] Not as "meaning", and so the definition is not necessarily exclusive in effect.

[2] 1936 Act, s. 343 (1).

[3] Act of 1950, s. 1 (3).

[4] *Smith v. West Dudley Local Board* (1878), 3 C. P. D. 423, and *Shoreditch Corporation v. Bull* (1904), 68 J.P. 415.

[5] *See, e. g., Kimber v. Gas Light & Coke Co.*, [1918] 1 K.B. 439.

[6] "Sewer" for present purposes, includes manholes and manhole covers: *Winslow v. Bushey U.D.C.* (1908), 72 J.P. 259. Whether or not street gullies leading to a sewer (as distinct from a mere highway drain) form part of the sewer or part of the highway is, apparently, a question of fact: *Papworth v. Battersea Corporation* (No. 2), [1916] 1 K.B. 583.

liable for any damage arising as a consequence of such lack of maintenance, suffered by a lawful user of the street, and the former principle of freedom from liability for "non-feasance" applied only to a highway authority acting as such (even where the sewer authority were also the highway authority).[1] On the other hand, if the sewer itself is properly laid and maintained, liability will not attach to the sewer authority as a consequence only of the presence of the sewer in the highway, as it is there under the authority of statute.[2] If a highway is mis-used (*e.g.*, by driving an exceptionally heavey vehicle along it in circumstances amounting to negligence), and a sewer under the highway, properly laid and protected, is thereby damaged it seems that the sewer authority will be able to recover damages from the person responsible in respect thereof.[3]

(ii) *To construct a public sewer in, or over any land not forming part of a street, after giving a reasonable notice to every owner and occupier of that land.*

It will be noticed that the somewhat awkward phrase, which was inserted in parenthesis in section 16 of the 1875 Act (the predecessor in title of the present section) to the effect that the power was to be exercisable only where the local authority's surveyor had stated that the passing through the private land in question

---

[1] *See, e.g., Skilton v. Epsom and Ewell U.D.C.*, [1936] 2 All E.R. 50.

[2] Such an action must be based on negligence: *Lambert v. Lowestoft Corporation* [1901] 1 K.B. 590, and *Thompson v. Brighton Corporation*, [1894] 1 Q.B. 332. Similar considerations will apply if a sewer is laid in the bed of a watercourse; but no liability can attach to the sewer authority if the sewer is initially properly laid but subsequently obstructs the flow of water in the river due to some change in the river not the responsibility of the sewer authority: *Radstock Co-operative and Industrial Society Co. Ltd. v. Norton-Radstock U.D.C.*, [1968] 2 All E.R. 59.

[3] *Driscoll v. Poplar Board of Works* (1897), 62 J.P. 40. The sewer authority may be able to sue the highway authority where their sewer is damaged by the use of exceptionally heavy equipment for highway repairs: see *Gas Light & Coke Co. v. Vestry of St. Mary Abbots* (1885), 15 Q.B.D. 1.

was necessary,[1] does not appear in the present section, and therefore only reasonable notice on the owner[2] and the occupier need be served.[3] The form of notice is immaterial, and there is no rule of thumb for judging what is "reasonable". The notice should be in writing,[4] and as long a notice as is practicable should be given. The section seems to give the authority an absolute discretion (especially in view of the deletion of the words in parenthesis in the former section above referred to) as to the course the sewer is to follow.[5] "Land" in the 1936 Act includes "any interest in land and any easement or right in, to or over land."[6]

A public sewer constructed under the present paragraph need not of necessity (though this will normally be the case) lead at either end (or at both ends) to a public sewer; it may be constructed so as to serve as a link between two private sewers,[7] although presumably the authority must in such a case acquire rights from the owner of at least one of the private sewers to allow the effluent from the public sewer to flow through that private sewer.

Where the construction of a sewer necessarily involved the demolition of a building, it was held in

---

[1] See, e.g., Lewis v. Weston-super-Mare Local Board (1888), 40 Ch. D. 55.

[2] As defined in s. 343 (1) of the 1936 Act, and see Chap. 11, post, p. 186. If there is any doubt of his identity, the water authority should first serve a "requisition for information" under s. 277 of the Act, applied by s. 14 (2) of the Water Act, 1973; post, p. 174.

[3] Service must be effected in accordance with s. 285 of the 1936 Act; post, p. 174.

[4] 1936 Act, s. 283. The notice should be sufficiently detailed to enable the recipient to appreciate exactly the proposals of the authority, but the route of the proposed sewer need not necessarily be accompanied by a plan (Cleckheaton Industrial Self-Help Society v. Jackson (1866), 14 W. R. 950). The sewer need not necessarily be laid underground: see Morris v. Mynyddislwyn U.D.C. [1917] 2 K.B. 309. Shaw's Form PH 85 is appropriate for this notice.

[5] Earl Derby v. Bury Commissioners (1869), L.R. 4 Ex. 222.

[6] See definition in s. 343 (1).

[7] Moore v. Frimley and Camberley U.D.C. (1965) 63 L.G.R. 194.

Hutton v. Esher U.D.C.[1] that the power given by section 15 was wide enough to cover such an operation. The Court of Appeal reached this conclusion by applying the definition of land in section 3 of the Interpretation Act, 1889[2] that there was insufficient indication in the statute to exclude that definition in this context. A right of water to a mill is, apparently also "land" for this purpose.[3]

No land need be acquired in order to lay a sewer under this section, and the procedure of the Acquisition of Land (Authorisation Procedure) Act, 1946, need not, therefore, be observed if a recalcitrant landowner objects to the laying of a sewer through his land; a notice under the present section alone is necessary.[4] The right to lay a sewer under this section, when exercised, however, has the effect of a compulsory acquisition of land, and entitles the landowner (and the occupier, in a proper case) to claim compensation, to be assessed (in case of dispute) by the Lands Tribunal in accordance with the principles of the Land Compensation Act, 1961 (consolidating earlier legislation),[5] and subject also to the special rule contained in section 278 (4) of the 1936 Act (applied by s. 14 (2) of the Water Act, 1973; *see* Chap. 11, *post*, p. 180). In addition to the claim for compensation, any person affected by

---

[1] [1973] 2 All E.R. 1123.

[2] "The expression 'land' shall include messuages, tenements, and hereditaments, houses, and buildings of any tenure", this definition being read as supplementing that in s. 343 (1) of the P.H.A. 1936 (above). *See now* Sched. 1 to the Interpretation Act 1978, under which "land" includes buildings and other structures, land covered with water, and any estate, interest, easement, servitude or right in or over land."

[3] *Cleckheaton U.D.C. v. Firth* (1898), 62 J.P. 536.

[4] *Thornton v. Nutter* (1867), 31 J.P. 419. The authority can enforce their right of entry pursuant to the powers given in s. 287 of the 1936 Act.

[5] *Thurrock Grays and Tilbury Joint Sewerage Board v. Thames Land Co., Ltd* (1926), 90 J.P. 1, explaining the effect of the earlier leading case of *Taylor v. Oldham Corporation* (1876), 4 Ch. D. 395. Under the 1936 Act, there is a specific duty to make compensation to any individual who has sustained damage by reason of the exercise by an authority of any of their functions (including the present) under the Act; *see* s. 278, and *post*, p. 182.

negligent or unlawful action on the part of the water authority in the course of laying the sewer, will be entitled to recover damages by ordinary action.[1]

A notice served under s. 15 may be withdrawn at any time before the work of constructing the public sewer is commenced, and in such a case no claim for compensation can arise.[2]

If the water authority propose to carry out sewage works under this section, they must (in addition to the notices served on landowners) give notice of their proposals to any parish or community (in Wales) council or to the parish meeting concerned.[3]

(iii) *To construct sewage disposal works.*[4]

(iv) *To acquire by agreement any sewer or sewage disposal works or the right to use any sewer or sewage disposal works.*

This power relates to existing sewers; it will be noted that the power does not extend to the acquisition of drains. The pargraph does not confer any right of compulsory acquisition.

General Observations.

In exercising their powers under this section, the water authority must do so in such a manner as not to create a nuisance. This general principle is given statutory effect by section 31 of the 1936 Act, and is an extension of the principle recognised in the leading case of *Metropolitan Asylums Board v. Hill,*[5] that where a statute confers a power (as distinct from a duty), such power must, if possible, be exercised in such a manner as not to cause a nuisance or infringe private rights.

---

[1] *E.g., Hardaker v. Idle U.D.C.,* [1896] 1 Q.B. 335.
[2] *Davis v. Witney U.D.C.* (1899) 63 J.P. 279.
[3] P.H.A., 1936, s. 15 (4).
[4] *See* Chap. 7, *post,* p. 102.
[5] (1881), 6 App. Cas. 193.

Where this provision is incorporated in the enabling statute itself, as here, the effect is to limit the power, so as to render it exercisable only if its exercise is possible without causing a nuisance.[1] The discharge of sewage into the sea may render the authority liable under the present provision,[2] and so may the pollution of a river by sewage.[3] If the water authority continue to operate an unsatisfactory system of sewage constructed by a private individual, they will not normally be liable in respect of any nuisance caused thereby, if they have not themselves altered the system in any way; a person aggrieved in such a case may be able to complain to the Secretary of State under section 322 of the 1936 Act.[4]

The 1936 Act does not in any way authorise the construction or use of any public or other sewer to convey any untreated sewage into any stream, pond, lake, etc.[5] The authority intending to construct a sewer must also, where relevant, obtain the consent of any person entitled to water rights who would be affected

---

[1] *See, e.g., Price's Patent Candle Co., Ltd. v. London County Council* [1908] 2 Ch. 526.

[2] *Hobart v. Southend-on-Sea Corporation* (1906), 75 L.H.K.B. 305, and *see post*, p. 115.

[3] *See* Chap. 8, *post*, p. 109.

[4] *Earl of Harrington v. Derby Corporation*, [1905] 1 Ch. 205; a local sanitary authority was not in these circumstances to be held liable for mere acts of neglect, the proper remedy in respect thereof being by way of complaint to the Secretary of State under s. 322. As section 15 of the 1936 Act is a function exercisable by a water authority, it seems that s. 322 will apply thereto (and it does not apply to s. 14 of the 1973 Act: *ante* p. 32). It will be observed, however, that in this and the previous cases on the point, the sewer in question vested in the local authority by operation of statute. It is doubtful whether a similar exemption from liability would be permitted by the courts where the particular sewer in question had been adopted by the authority under s. 17 of the 1936 Act, the authority in such a case having taken (by virtue of such adoption) some positive action with regard to the sewer. On the other hand, the authority will not be liable in damages for nuisances caused by their sewerage system becoming overloaded or surcharged owing to premises being connected thereto, as the authority cannot prevent such connections, by virtue of s. 34 of the 1936 Act: *Smeaton v. Ilford Corporation* [1954] 1 All E.R. 923.

[5] *See* 1936 Act, s. 30 and Chap. 8, *post*, p. 109.

thereby,[1] of any dock undertakers concerned,[2] of the British Railways Board where appropriate,[3] and of any land drainage authorities who are concerned in any such proposals.[4] In addition notice of the proposals must be served on the following:

(*a*) Any land drainage authority in whom a watercourse or works is vested, which will be crossed or interfered with by the proposed sewer.[5] Any such authority may within 28 days serve notice of objection on the local authority, and the works may not then be proceeded with until either such objections are withdrawn, or the Secretary of State has approved the proposals, after holding a local inquiry.[6]

(*b*) Where appropriate, the parish council or community council in Wales (or parish meeting if there is no parish council) of each parish or community to be served by the proposed works.[7] The parish council (or meeting) have no specific right of objection under the section, but they could make a complaint (as "a person aggrieved") to the Secretary of State under section 322 of the 1936 Act in an appropriate case.

3.   THE RECOVERY OF EXPENSES.

As a general rule, it being the duty of the water authority to sewer their area, an authority cannot recover the cost of constructing a public sewer or any portion thereof from any landowner or other individual

---

[1] 1936 Act, s. 331.
[2] 1936 Act, s. 333.
[3] *Ibid.*, and Transport Acts, 1947 and 1962.
[4] 1936 Act, s. 334.
[5] 1936 Act, s. 15 (2).
[6] 1936 Act, s. 15 (3).
[7] 1936 Act, s. 15 (4). as amended by the Local Government Act 1972 and the Water Act 1973.

who may benefit from that sewer. There has always been one exception to that general principle, namely where the sewer is constructed as part of a private street works scheme,[1] but under the Act of 1961, there are two further exceptions which do not depend on the construction of a sewer in a private street.[2]

The special powers (available after 1974 to the water authority) to recover contributions under the 1961 Act apply to

(a) cases where a sewer is constructed in a highway maintainable at the public expense,[3] and to

(b) cases where land in which a sewer has been laid after 3rd October 1961,[4] has subsequently been laid out as a street.[5]

In any case where the first of these provisions apply, the construction of the sewer must be completed within two years of the resolution to construct the sewer. If in a particular case construction had not been started within the two years, there seems to be no reason why the water authority should not pass (and advertise) a new resolution. The authority must resolve (in case (a) or (b) above) that in their opinion the construction of the sewer in question will, or (in a case under (b) above) has, increase(d) the value of the premises fronting the street. Notice of this resolution must be published in a local newspaper,[6] and if payments are to be recoverable from frontagers to the street, the pro-

---

[1] This work would still be carried out by the county council, not the water authority: see Chapter 6, post, page 98.

[2] It has always been anomalus that the power to recover contributions depended on the status of the street, and not on the importance of the sewer.

[3] 1961 Act, s. 12. As to such highways, see Highways Act, 1980, section 36.

[4] The date of commencement of the 1961 Act: s. 86 (2) (b).

[5] Section 13.

[6] Section 12 (2) or 13 (2).

cedure set out in the Second Schedule to the 1961 Act must be followed.

This provides that a notice must be served on owners of premises fronting[1] the street, specifying

(a) the amount of the actual cost per yard of the sewer constructed in the street, and

(b) the amount which the local authority estimate as the cost per yard of a sewer having an internal diameter of nine inches constructed in the street at a depth of seven feet.

Within one month any person on whom such a notice is served may object to the water authority, who may then refer the objection to the local magistrates' court for their determination. When a notice has so been served, and subject to any order varying the terms of the notice made by the magistrates, any frontager may become liable to pay a contribution to the cost of constructing the sewer assessed at **one-half** of the **actual** cost per yard of the sewer, or the **estimated** cost of a sewer of an internal diameter of nine inches constructed in that street at a depth of seven feet, whichever is the *less*, and multiplied by the extent in yards of the frontage of the premises.[2] However, such a contribution will not become recoverable by the water authority unless and until a building is erected on premises fronting the street in which the sewer is or has been laid, **after** the operative date of the authority's resolution under the section, and also provided that the building is connected with the sewer for the purpose of discharging foul water.[3] In such event, a payment may be recovered by the water authority from the owner of the premises "for the time being". When these charges

---

[1] An expression which includes adjoining and abutting: Second Schedule, para. 7 (1).
[2] 1961 Act, s. 12 (6).
[3] *Ibid.*, s. 12 (5).

were recoverable by the **local** authority (before 1974), it seems than an entry ought to have been made in the local land charges register in respect thereof, and this now applies to charges acquired by a water authority.[1]

Apart from these provisions, any contribution from a private individual towards the cost of constructing a public sewer by a water authority is a matter of private negotiation. If for example, a private developer requests the water authority to extend a public sewer to enable him to drain his estate, the procedure of section 16 (above, page 34) of the Water Act 1973 will apply.

It may also be observed that in such a case it is not proper, when a local planning authority grants planning permission for such development, to impose a condition to the effect that the developer shall cause his estate drains to be connected to a public sewer at his expense; this is not a valid condition,[2] as this is a matter which is capable of being controlled under the 1936 Act.[3]

It may be a valid reason to withhold planning permission because adequate provision cannot be made for the sewerage of an extensive development and planning authorities should consult with water authorities on such applications, but absence of main sewerage is almost certainly not a good reason for refusing planning permission for the erection of a single house.[4]

4. THE CONSTRUCTION OF SEWERS AND PLANNING.

The construction of a sewer, whether by a water authority or by a private individual, being the carrying

---

[1] Local Land Charges Act 1975, s. 1 (1).
[2] *See Hall v. Shoreham-on-Sea U.D.C.,* [19642] 1 All E.R. 1.
[3] The local authority will not be entitled to require him to connect to any public sewer not within 100 feet of his property: Chapter 9, *post*, page 129.
[4] *See* articles by the present author at [1961] J.P.L. 84 and [1959] J.P.L. 236.

out of "engineering, mining or other operations in, on, over or under land," falls within the definition of "development" for the purposes of the Town and Country Planning Act, 1971, and therefore express planning permission for the construction of sewers and drains (other than as an integral part of some development for which permission has been obtained) is necessary.[1] However, in the case of development by a water authority or a new town development corporation or being "development not above ground level required in connection with the provision, improvement or maintenance of sewers", express planning permission is not necessary, as such development is covered by Class XVII of the Town and Country Planning General Development Order, 1977.[2] The erection, construction or placing of buildings, plants or apparatus (including, for example, ventilating shafts) on land by water authorities, is covered by Class XVI, *ibid*. These provisions do not, however, affect the construction of sewers by private individuals and those will require express planning permission in the ordinary manner.[3]

No special steps under the planning legislation have to be taken in connection with the laying of sewers, as distinct from the construction of sewage works.[4]

5. SEWER RECORDS.

Under section 32 of the 1936 Act, it is the duty of the distict council (**not** the water authority) or London Borough Council to keep deposited at their offices a map,[5] for inspection by any person at all reasonable

---

[1] *See* s. 22 (1) thereof.

[2] S.I. 1977 No. 289.

[3] *I.e.*, in accordance with the Town and Country Planning General Development Order, 1977.

[4] *See* Chap. 7, *post*, p. 102.

[5] The scale is not specified, and any adequate scale sufficient to show necessary detail may be used; most authorities use maps to the scale 1/2250 (25 in. to mile).

hours free of charge, which shows and distinguishes "all sewers and drains"[1] within their district which are:

    (i) Public sewers, except those which were vested in the local authority on the 1st October, 1937,[2] unless they were reserved for foul water only or for surface water only,[3] in which case they must be shown on the map regardless of the date of vesting;

    (ii) Sewers with respect to which a vesting declaration under section 17 of the Act[4] has been made, but has not yet taken effect;

    (iii) Sewers or drains with respect to which an agreement to make a vesting declaration in the future has been entered into under section 18 of the Act.[5]

In addition, where it is the practice to reserve certain sewers for foul water only or for surface water only,[6] the map must show the purposes which each such sewer is intended to serve.[7]

The council of every inner London borough, and the Common Council of the City must supply a copy of the sewer map for their area to the Greater London Council.[8]

The duty to keep such a map is one which is, presumably, enforceable by *mandamus*, and it would seem that any person aggrieved by any error in a map (where, *e.g.*, by the failure to show a particular sewer,

---

[1] Only sewers can be vested as public sewers, but an agreement may be made under s. 18 in respect of a drain, which will not be effective until that drain has become a sewer.
[2] The date of commencement of the 1936 Act: s. 347 (1).
[3] Under s. 22; *see post*, p. 80.
[4] *See* Chap. 4, *post*, p. 57.
[5] *See* Chap. 4, *post*, p. 62.
[6] Under s. 22; *see post*, p. 80.
[7] 1936 Act, s. 32 (2).
[8] 1936 Act, s. 32 (4).

the complainant has incurred abortive expenditure) would have an action in negligence for damages against the local authority. It is also in the interests of the authority to maintain this map correctly, for it is only those public sewers which are shown thereon over which the authority has control in respect of buildings without consent.[1]

---

[1] 1936 Act, s. 25; Chap. 5, *post*, p. 82.

CHAPTER 4

CONSTRUCTION OF SEWERS BY PRIVATE INDIVIDUALS[1]

1. INTRODUCTORY.

The construction of a drain or sewer for the purpose of draining one's land or premises is a natural incident of the ownership of that land. Thus, where a land-owner, without negligence and by proper methods, constructed a drain on his own land, but as a consequence of the necessary excavations set natural agencies in motion which drained off subterranean water from underneath neighbouring land and caused the surface thereof to subside, he was held not liable in damages in respect thereof.[2] Once the landowner has caused sewage or other matter to collect on his land (in the drain pipes, or in a cesspool or tank), he will be held liable if he allows such matter to escape.[3] Liability under this principle—an application of the famous "Rule in *Rylands v. Fletcher*"—will attach irrespective of the proof of any negligence or even any knowledge

---

[1] The expression "private individual" is used in this Chapter as including any body incorporate other than a local or water authority.
[2] *Popplewell v. Hodkinson* (1869), L.R. 4 Exch. 248; it was an essential feature of the case that the natural agencies in question could not reasonably have been foreseen.
[3] *Rylands v. Fletcher* (1868), L.R. 3 H.L. 330; *see e.g., Jones v. Bedwellty U.D.C.* (1916), 80 J.P. Jo. 192. "I think it clear that the principle of *Rylands v. Fletcher* would apply to the owner of a sewer, whether he himself made the sewer or not. . . . His duty at common law would be to see that the sewage in his sewer did not escape to the injury of others": *per Parker, J., in Jones v. Llanrwst U.D.C.*, [1911] 1 Ch. 393.

of the cause of the occurrence resulting in the damage complained of.[1]

The right to cause sewage matter to flow under or across another's land is thus one which must be acquired by prescription[2] or express grant. The details of such matters form part of the law of easements; in the present context we are concerned rather with relations between the water authority or (in some instances) the local authority and a private individual proposing to construct a sewer[3]; the construction of drains by private individuals is considered later.[4]

It is perhaps here relevant to observe that sewers are now completely exempt from rating,[5] but privately owned sewers are subject to income tax.[6]

2. THE CONSTRUCTION OF PRIVATE SEWERS.

There is no express provision in the 1936 Act requiring a private individual proposing to construct a sewer to submit plans thereof to, or to obtain the approval of, the local or the water authority, but such

---

[1] As in *Humphries v. Cousins* (1877), 2 C.P.D. 239; "It was the defendant's duty to keep the sewage which he was himself bound to receive from passing from his own premises to the plaintiff's premises, otherwise than along the old accustomed channel": *per* Denman, J., at p. 244.

[2] *See ante*, Chap. 2, p. 29.

[3] A private individual has none of the special powers (local or private Acts apart) of the local authority discussed in Chap. 3, *ante*, p. 32, *et seq.* Thus, the breaking up of the surface of a street for the purpose of laying a private sewer (as distinct from making a communication with a public sewer: *see* s. 34 (2) of the 1936 Act) may be done only by agreement with the highway or other appropriate authority.

[4] *See* Chap. 9, *post*, p. 117. The difference between private sewers and private drains is that between sewers and drains generally; *see* Chap. 1, *ante*, p. 1, and Chap. 2, p. 15.

[5] General Rate Act 1968, s. 42; the section exempts from rating all "sewers" as defined by s. 343 (1) of the 1936 Act and s. 81 of the Public Health (London) Act, 1936. The exemption also applies to any "manhole, ventilating shaft, pumping station, pump or other accessory belonging to such a sewer".

[6] Local authorities are totally exempt from income tax (Income and Corporation Taxes Act, 1970, s. 353), and presumably this applies to water authorities at least so far as sewerage functions are concerned (Water Act 1973, s. 14 (2)).

proposals are in effect regulated as a consequence of the following provisions:

(a) New Buildings.

Satisfactory provision must be made for the drainage[1] of any new building, and the plans required to be submitted under the Building Regulations 1976 (administered by the local authority) in respect thereof must be rejected if such provision is not shown to be made.[2] Obviously, it is in the interests of any landowner carrying out an extensive private sewerage scheme to obtain the prior approval of the authority to any such proposals, otherwise he may find when he proposes to connect new buildings thereto, that the new sewers so provided are not considered to provide a satisfactory means of drainage of such buildings.[3]

(b) Existing Buildings.

If any private sewer or drain[4] of an existing building is "insufficient",[5] or, in the case of a sewer or drain communicating directly or indirectly with a public sewer, is so defective as to admit subsoil water, or if it is in such a condition as to be prejudicial to health or a nuisance,[6] the local authority may, in any such case, require[7] the defect to be remedied or the nuisance abated, and, in the event of their requirements not being complied with, they may themselves act in default and

---

[1] As defined in s. 37 of the 1936 Act, *i.e.*, including "the conveyance, by means of a sink and any other necessary appliance, of refuse water and the conveyance of rain water from roofs."

[2] 1936 Act, s. 37; *see post*, p. 128.

[3] Unfortunately, as there is no express provision requiring such approval to be obtained, any observations of the authority on such proposals could be but informal, and would not be legally binding on the authority. As to connections with existing public sewers, *see* ss. 34 and 36 of the 1936 Act, Chap. 9, *post*, p. 118.

[4] Or cesspool, soil pipe, rain water pipe, spout, sink or other necessary appliance: 1936 Act, s. 39; *post*, Chap. 9, p. 138.

[5] This term is not defined or explained in the Act, but *see post*, p. 137.

[6] As to the effect of this phrase see *post*, page 141.

[7] By notice signed by an authorised officer (s. 284), and duly served (s. 285). There is no prescribed form, but *see* Shaw's Form PN 23D.

recover their expenses in so doing as a charge on the property or be demanded from the owner of the property for the time being.[1] This section forms, in practice, a most effective means of control by the local authority over the condition etc., of private drains and sewers.

(c) Special Cases.

The water authority may, in certain circumstances, require[2] any person[3] proposing to construct a drain or sewer, so to construct it in manner differing ("as regards material or size of pipes, depth, fall, direction or outfall or otherwise"[4]) from that in which he proposes, to the specification of the authority.[5] This power may be exercised by the authority only when they consider[6] that the "proposed drain or sewer is, or is likely to be, needed to form part of a general sewerage system which they have provided or propose to provide".[5]

In any such case, failure to comply with the authority's requirements renders the offender liable to criminal proceedings, but if he considers himself aggrived by those requirements, he may, within 28 days,[7] appeal to the Secretary of State.[8]

---

[1] 1936 Act, ss. 39 and 291, and *post*, Chap. 11, p. 186.

[2] By notice signed by an authorised officer (s. 284), and duly served (s. 285). There is no prescribed form, but *see* Shaw's Form PN 7.

[3] "Person" here must include a county council, and therefore it seems that a water authority may take action under this section against the county council acting under the private street works code contained in the Highways Act, 1980.

[4] The words "or otherwise" normally suggest that the *ejusdem generis* rule is to be applied, but it is submitted that the rule is not applicable in the present context, as the terms used are of different *genera* (*see, e.g., R. v. Payne* (1866), 35 L.J.M.C. 170, and *Maxwell on the Interpretation of Statutes*, 11th edn., p. 333).

[5] 1936 Act, s. 19 (1).

[6] Provided there are reasonable grounds on which the authority could come to such a decision, it seems that the courts could not intervene to question the actual decision.

[7] Presumably the 28 days will have to be calculated as from the date of the notice specifying the authority's requirements.

[8] There is no specified procedure for such appeals, but under s. 318 the Secretary of State may decide to hold a public local inquiry into the matter of any appeal to him.

Any person who alters his scheme of construction of a private drain or sewer to meet the requirements of the water authority is entitled to reimbursement by them of any extra expenses he reasonably incurs in complying with such requirements, and also from time to time, of so much of any expenses reasonably incurred by him in repairing or maintaining the drain or sewer as may be attributable to the authority's requirements having been made and complied with.[1] Any question as to the amount of such expenses is to be determined by the local magistrates' court or (at the option of the person entitled to reimbursement as aforesaid) by arbitration.[2]

If any person[3] reconstructs an existing drain, or executes works of any kind so as permanently to discontinue the use of a drain, he must cause any drains or parts of drains thereby becoming disused or unnecessary to be disconnected and sealed at such points as the local authority may reasonable require,[4] and he must give at least 48 hours notice to the local authority before complying with this requirement.[5] The local authority are not given any powers to take action themselves in default of compliance with this provision, but failure to give the notice referred to renders the offender liable to a fine on conviction. In the case of a demolition of a building, the local authority have further powers of control.[6]

(d) Planning Control.

Direct detailed control over the construction of private sewerage or drainage schemes is maintained under

---

[1] 1936 Act, s. 19 (2).

[2] References to an arbitrator under this provision are to a single arbitrator appointed by agreement between the parties, or, in default of agreement, by the Secretary of State: 1936 Act, s. 303; and *see* Chap. 11, *post*, p. 184.

[3] The section applies to any person, including apparently a contractor, and it is not confined to cases where a new sewer is being constructed.

[4] 1961 Act, s. 19 (1).

[5] *Ibid.*, s. 19 (4).

[6] 1961 Act, s. 29.

the Town and Country Planning Act, 1971, enforceable by the local planning authority who in this case will probably be the district council, except in a case of a major scheme considered to be a "county planning matter" (see Local Government Act 1972), Schedule 16).

Under this Act the construction of such works, being engineering operations in, on or over land, amounts to development,[1] and as such needs the express permission of the local planning authority.

(e) Other Provisions.
The general law affords no obstacles to the construction of a private sewer or drain thereto, provided any necessary easements or other rights can be obtained from other landowners, and no common law nuisance is caused as a result. If it is intended to connect a new drain or private sewer to an existing *private* drain or sewer, the consent of the owners of the land through which that existing conduit runs must be obtained. The owner of the land from which the existing effluent originates will have obtained an easement and the burden thereby placed on the servient owner cannot be increased without his consent.[2]

The construction of works for the supply of sewage to land for agricultural purposes is deemed to be an improvement of land within the Improvement of Land Act, 1864,[3] and the construction of sewers and drainage is an authorised improvement, the cost of which may be expended out of capital moneys and is not liable to be replaced by instalments under the Settled Land Act, 1925.[4]

The institution of an efficient sanitary system for a

---

[1] *See* definition of "development" in s. 22 of the 1971 Act.
[2] See such cases as *Bracewell v. Appleby* [1975] 1 All E.R. 993.
[3] 1936 Act, s. 33.
[4] Settled Land Act, 1925, s. 83, and Third Schedule, Part I.

dwellinghouse will constitute an "improvement" for the purposes of the Rent Act in the case of a controlled tenancy,[1] as will the construction of sewers as part of private street works.[2]

3. THE ADOPTION OF SEWERS.

Provided the appropriate procedure is followed, the water authority may at any time "adopt" any sewer,[3] or any part thereof,[4] or any sewage disposal works, situate within their area, the construction whereof was not completed before the 1st October, 1937.[5]

(a) Effect of a Declaration.

The effect of any such declaration (which may be in the form of an ordinary resolution of the authority) is to cause the sewer to vest in the authority as from the date of such declaration.[6] It should be noted, however, that any person who, immediately before the making of a vesting declaration, was entitled to use the sewer, shall be entitled to use it (or any sewer substituted therefor), to the same extent as if the declaration had not been made.[7] A water authority in whom a sewer improperly or negligently constructed had vested by virtue of a statute[8] "whether with or against their will", would probably not be liable for any damage caused as a consequence of such faulty construction, even where the same occurred subsequent to the vesting of the sewer in the authority,[9] but it would seem that this immunity from liability would not protect an authority

---

[1] *Strood Estates Co. Ltd. v. Gregory*, [1938] A.C. 118.
[2] Rent Act, 1977, s. 34.
[3] The provision applies only to sewers, not to drains; but *see also* s. 18 of the 1936 Act, *post*, p. 62.
[4] 1936 Act, s. 17 (6).
[5] 1936 Act, s. 17. The date mentioned was the date of commencement of the 1936 Act: *see* s. 347 (1) thereof.
[6] *Cf.* Chap. 2, *ante*, p. 11.
[7] 1936 Act, s. 17 (5).
[8] *E.g.,* under s. 13 of the 1875 Act; *ante*, p. 12.
[9] *Morris v. Mynyddislwyn U.D.C.*, [1917] 2 K.B. 309.

who had adopted a defective private sewer under the present provision, as in such circumstances they could be held to have taken positive action with regard to the sewer.

(b) Procedure.

When an authority propose to adopt a sewer by a declaration of vesting under the section,[1] the following procedure must be observed:

(i) Notice[2] of the proposal must be given to the owners of the sewer or works in question.

(ii) In the rare case where the sewer, etc., in question is situate outside the area of the "adopting" water authority, they must give notice[3] of their proposal to the authority in whose area the sewer is situate, and may not proceed to make the vesting declaration until *either* the other authority has consented thereto, *or* the Secretary of State, on application to him, has[4] "dispensed with the necessity for such consent, either unconditionally or subject to such conditions as he may think fit to impose".[5]

(iii) No vesting declaration may be made (except

---

[1] The owner himself may make application to the authority for a declaration to be made (1936 Act, s. 17 (2)); in any such case, the authority should make its decision on such application within two months (*see* note [10] on p. 59). It is suggested that a declaration of vesting should be made in respect of the sewers on any new private estate when the building has been completed, provided of course the sewers have been properly constructed. Where the sewers can be said to form part of a street, adoption of the street may include adoption of the sewer, but in any case of doubt the procedure of the present section should be followed.

[2] The notice must be in writing, signed by the appropriate authorised officer (1936 Act, s. 284), and must be served in the prescribed manner (*ibid.*, s. 285). The notice itself need not be in any particular form, but Shaw's Form PN 4 is appropriate.

[3] *See* preceding note; the same notice will serve for this purpose also.

[4] No provision is made in the section for an inquiry, but the Secretary of State has power to convene one under s. 318 of the 1936 Act.

[5] 1936 Act, s. 17 (7).

on the application of such body) in respect of any sewer, or of any part thereof, which is vested in another water authority, a county council,[1] board,[2] the British Railways Board,[3] or any dock undertakers.[4]

When the notice under (i) above has been served, the adopting water authority may not proceed further in the matter until **either** two months[5] have elapsed[6] without an appeal against the authority's proposals being lodged,[7] **or** until any such appeal has been determined.[8] Any owner[9] aggrieved by the proposal of the authority to make a vesting declaration, may appeal to the Secretary of State within two months[3] after the notice of the proposal was served upon him; and a similar right of appeal is open to any owner who is aggrieved by the refusal of a water authority to make a vesting declaration under the section on his application.[10]

The relationship between "adoption" and the other means (in particular s. 20 (1) (*b*)) whereby a sewer may become a public sewer, should not be overlooked. Thus, in the following diagram, the whole of the drainage system serving the 13 houses in Lovers' Close (having been constructed after 1936 by a private developer)

---

[1] This will be of particular importance with reference to highway sewers: *see* Chap. 6, *post*, p. 91.

[2] This term includes a joint committee; *see* s. 90 (1) of the 1936 Act.

[3] Transport Acts, 1947 and 1962.

[4] Provided the sewer, etc., in question is situate in or on land which belongs to them and is held or used by them for the purposes of their undertaking. "Dock undertakers" is defined for the purposes of the 1936 Act in s. 343 (1) thereof.

[5] *I.e.*, two calender months: Interpretation Act, 1978, Sched. 1.

[6] Presumably, from the date of service of the notice.

[7] *See* below, note [10].

[8] 1936 Act, s. 17 (1).

[9] Presumably, this means the owner of the sewer, etc., in question; "owner" is defined for the purposes of the 1936 Act in s. 343 (1) thereof.

[10] This right of appeal may be exercised at any time after he has received notice of the authority's refusal of his application, or, if he receives no such notice, at any time after the expiration of two months from the making of his application (1936 Act, s. 17 (3)).

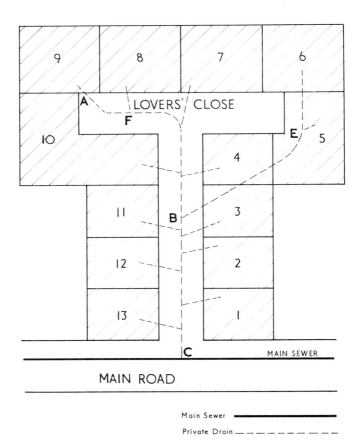

could be adopted by the water authority by resolution under s. 17; the lengths F-C and E-B would then become public sewers. On the other hand if the roadway of Lovers' Close is made up under the private street works code (Highways Act, 1980, Part XI), the sewers in the highway (*i.e.*, length F-C) alone will vest in the water authority under s. 20 (1) (*b*), leaving length E-B as a private sewer.

(c) Refusal or failure to make a declaration.

When the water authority consider the question whether to make a vesting declaration with regard to a particular sewer, etc., or when the Secretary of State considers an appeal under the section, regard must be had to all the circumstances of the case, but the following matters must specifically be taken into account[1]:

" (i) Whether the sewer, or works in question is or are adapted to, or required for, any general system of sewerage or sewage disposal which the authority have provided, or propose to provide, for their district or any part thereof;

(ii) Whether the sewer is constructed under a highway or under land reserved by a planning scheme[2] for a street;

(iii) The number of buildings which the sewer is intended to serve, and whether, regard being had to the proximity of other buildings or the prospect of future development,

---

[1] 1936 Act, s. 17 (4).

[2] This expression was not deleted from the present section by the Town and Country Planning Act, 1947 or by any corresponding provisions in the Town and Country Planning Act, 1971; but it is submitted that it must be understood to refer to a confirmed development plan under the 1971 Act. It should be noted that the definition of "planning scheme" in s. 343 (1) of the 1936 Act was repealed by the Ninth Schedule of the Town and Country Planning Act, 1947.

it is likely to be required to serve additional buildings;

(iv) The method of construction and state of repair of the sewer or works; **and**

(v) In a case where an owner objects, whether the making of the proposed vesting declaration would be seriously detrimental[1] to him.''

On an appeal,[2] either against the proposals of the authority to make a declaration, or their refusal to make a declaration, the Secretary of State may allow or disallow the authority's proposals, or may make any declaration the authority might have made. In addition, he may specify conditions (including conditions as to the payment of compensation[3] by the water authority), and may direct that any declaration he had made should not take effect unless any such conditions are accepted.[4]

4. AGREEMENTS FOR THE ADOPTION OF SEWERS.

Under section 18 of the 1936 Act, a water authority may agree with any person who is constructing or proposing to construct a sewer or sewage disposal works that, provided the sewer, etc., is constructed in manner

---

[1] There is no elucidation in the section of this somewhat obscure expression.

[2] Appeals may be lodged by simple letter addressed to the Department of the Environment; there are no rules of procedure governing their conduct, except that if the rules of "natural justice" were not observed on a particular appeal, the proceedings could presumably be quashed by the Courts.

[3] The authority themselves have no power to agree to make compensation to the owner, nor can they be compelled to do so, except on appeal to the Secretary of State. Even if the owner can prove that he has sustained damage as a consequence of the authority having exercised their powers under the section, any right to compensation (except through an appeal to the Secretary of State) is excluded specifically by s. 278 (3) of the 1936 Act (*post*, Chap. 11, p. 181).

[4] 1936 Act, s. 17 (3); the conditions must be accepted, presumably, by the appellant.

specified in the agreement, the authority will make a vesting declaration on completion of the work, or on some specified date. Any such agreement is expressly made enforceable against the water authority by the owner or occupier for the time being of any premises served by the sewer, etc.[1]

No agreement may be entered into under this section in respect of a sewer, etc., situate within the area of another water authority, until that authority has consented thereto or the Secretary of State has, on an application made to him, dispensed with the need for such consent.[2]

---

[1] 1936 Act, s. 18 (1).
[2] 1936 Act, s. 18 (3), and compare the power of the Secretary of State under s. 17 (7), *ante*, p. 57.

CHAPTER 5

MAINTENANCE AND USE OF PUBLIC SEWERS

1. THE GENERAL DUTIES OF WATER AUTHORITIES.

Under section 23 of the 1936 Act, it is made the duty of every water authority to "maintain, cleanse and empty", all public sewers vested in them.[1] In practice the section will frequently be administered by the local authority on behalf of the water authority, pursuant to "arrangements" made under section 15 of the Water Act, 1973.

For the purposes of the present section, it is submitted that "maintain" must include all ordinary works of repair,[2] and that "cleanse" must include the clearance of obstructions; "empty" must, it is submitted, mean that the authority are under a duty to provide and maintain a proper outfall,[3] and to cause the sewage or other contents of the sewer to flow in the direction of the outfall. The duty applies to all public sewers vested in the authority, whether or not laid through or under private land; as a necessary ancillary of the duty, it seems that the authority must be empowered to enter on any privately owned land in or through which the sewer is laid, for the purpose of executing their duties

---

[1] *See* Chap. 2, *ante*, p. 11, as to the vesting of sewers. This duty is in no way affected by any right the authority may have to recover their expenses in any particular case: *see* s. 24 of the 1936 Act, *post*, p. 70.

[2] The provision of new sewers will be covered by the duty imposed by s. 14 of the 1973 Act; Chap. 3, *ante*, p. 32.

[3] As to the duty to provide a proper outfall, *see R. v. Tynemouth R.D.C.*, [1896] 2 Q.B. 451.

under the present section.[1] This right of entry will, however, be strictly confined by the Courts to the minimum that is necessary for the authority's lawful purposes, and if the right is exceeded, the authority (and its servants) will be liable in damages as trespassers *ab initio*.[2]

The duty to "maintain" must not be taken too far; in *Radstock Co-operative Society v. Norton-Radstock U.D.C.*,[3] Ungoed-Thomas, J, said, at p. 825, "I fail to see that the statutory obligation to 'maintain' the sewer involves any such extended obligation to maintain lands or conditions outside the sewer, as the plaintiffs suggest, or that it involves obligations to third parties like the plaintiffs who are complete strangers to the sewer". In this case a public sewer had been properly constructed in a river bed, and in the course of time without any fault on the part of the local authority, the bed of the river became washed away and the sewer pipe became exposed, which caused eddies in the flow of water, which in turn damaged the plaintiffs' property. The plaintiffs claimed *inter alia* in nuisance, but were unsuccessful both at first instance and in the Court of Appeal.[4]

It is a matter for consideration, however, whether a water authority would be liable to a plaintiff injured by (for example) the defective state of a manhole cover[5] situate in private premises. They are obliged to observe the ordinary duty of care in respect of such a structure,[6] even if they were not aware of the existence of the

---

[1] *Birkenhead Corporation v. L.N.W.R. Co.* (1885), 15 Q.B.D. 572. The procedure of s. 287 of the Act must, however, be observed; *see* Chap. 11, *post*, p. 175.

[2] *The Six Carpenters' Case* (1610), 1 Sm. L.C. 134, and *cf.* "Freedom under the Law," by Lord Denning, at p. 112.

[3] [1967] 2 All E.R. 812; this point was not discussed in the Court of Appeal: *see* [1968] 2 All E.R. 59.

[4] [1968] 2 All E.R. 59.

[5] Which will normally form part of the sewer: P.H.A., 1936, s. 90 (4).

[6] Occupiers' Liability Act, 1957, s. 1 (3) (a), and s. 2 (2).

sewer itself, but it is not clear whether in such a case the courts would be prepared to hold an authority liable on the ground that they had not carried out any regular system of inspection of sewers on private property; presumably the case would turn on what was commonly accepted practice among sewer authorities in such cases.

The duty imposed under section 23 must be exercised by the authority in such manner as will not offend the other provisions of the Act, in particular, the following:

(i) All sewage or other noxious matter must be purified before it is discharged into streams, ponds, canals, etc.[1]

(ii) The authority must so execute their functions as not to create a nuisance.[2]

Normally speaking, the appropriate remedy open to a person aggrieved by the failure of a water authority to fulfil their duties under section 23[3] is by way of complaint to the Secretary of State under section 322 of the 1936 Act,[4] and not by action for negligence, for an injunction, or for a declaration, as the statute has specifically provided this procedure to meet cases of such dereliction of duty.[5]

No particular procedure regulates the making of such a complaint under the 1936 Act, and it seems that a complainant need not have any specific interest in the matter. Such a complaint may be made whenever the [water] authority "have failed to discharge their functions under this Act in any case where they ought to

---

[1] 1936 Act, s. 30, and see Chap. 8, *post*, p. 109.
[2] 1936 Act, s. 31.
[3] *See* s. 14 (2) of the 1973 Act.
[4] Unlike the duty to provide sewers under s. 14 of the 1973 Act, it seems that section 322 (which is included in Part XII of the 1936 Act) is to be read as applying to default by a water authority: see Water Act, 1973, s. 14 (2) (a) and the concluding words of s. 14 (2).
[5] *See, e.g., Pasmore v. Oswaldtwistle U.D.C.*, [1898] A.C. 387.

have done so".[1] The section would seem, therefore, to have excluded the jurisdiction of the courts in a case where the authority improperly fail to maintain a sewer, but civil proceedings for damages (either in negligence or for an injunction by the Attorney-General, at the relation of a person aggrieved) are not excluded if negligent or improper maintenance on the part of the authority can be alleged, or if the complaint is based on some positive action by the authority whereby legal rights have been infringed.[2]

The Tribunals and Inquiries Act, 1971, section 14 (1), provides that any provision in an Act that "any order or determination shall not be called into question in any court, or any provision in [an] Act which by similar words excludes any of the powers of the High Court, shall not have effect so as to" exclude the powers of the High Court to grant an order of *certiorari* or *mandamus*. *Certiorari* is not relevant, but *mandamus* is,[3] and it is of importance to consider whether the effect of this section is to give a person aggrieved the right to obtain a *mandamus*, as an alternative to making a complaint under section 322. It is submitted that the section does not have this effect, as there are no "sim-

---

[1] The Secretary of State may also take action under the section on his own initiative, without waiting for a complaint. "Functions" in this section includes powers and duties (*see* s. 343 (1)).

[2] Liability arises only if the authority are guilty of negligence or a breach of statutory duty (1936 Act, s. 30) in that they perform their duties in such a manner as to cause a nuisance. The suggestion that they are liable only for acts of misfeasance or malfeasance, as distinct from non-feasance, is not sound: *Pride of Derby v. British Celanese Ltd.*, [1953] Ch. 149; *Smeaton v. Ilford Corporation*, [1954] 1 All E.R. 923. Liability in trespass or negligence also is not excluded by the statute: *Dent v. Bournemouth Corporation* (1897), 66 L.J.Q.B. 395. For proceedings by the Attorney-General, based on nuisance, *see e.g., Attorney-General v. Halifax Corporation* (1869), 39 L.J. Ch. 129, *Attorney-General v. Ringwood R.D.C.* (1928), 92 J.P. 65, and *Jones v. Llanrwst U.D.C.* (1911), 80 L.J. Ch. 145. An action in nuisance can be brought in these circumstances, it seems, only if the defendant authority had notice thereof before the commencement of the action: *Cornford v. Havant and Waterloo U.D.C.* (1933), 97 J.P. 137.

[3] In s. 322 (2), the Secretary of State's power to enforce compliance with the section by an order of *mandamus*, as an alternative to the use of his default powers, is expressly reserved.

ilar words" in the section excluding the jurisdiction of
the courts. So the provision in the 1971 Act would
seem not to be relevant.

Under the provision of the 1875 Act[1] corresponding
to sections 23 and 31 of the 1936 Act it was suggested
that where the authority had been guilty of some defi-
nite act of negligence, whereby the plaintiff's private
rights had been injured and a nuisance had been
caused, an action would lie.[2] On the other hand, where
a particular system of drainage, which has vested in the
authority by virtue of some statutory provision,[3] is in-
capable of repair, the present provision cannot be invoked to compel (except by complaint to the Secretary
of State) the authority to carry out a scheme of
reconstruction.[4] The distinction between these two principles is often difficult to draw, but the following extract
from the judgment of Lord Halsbury, C., in *Baron v.
Portslade U.D.C.*[5] is helpful in this connection:–

> "Now there is all the difference in the world
> between the right to call on a local authority to
> make a new system of drainage and the right to
> compel them to use in a reasonable manner the
> sewers that are vested in them. No complaint has
> been made that the defendants ought to provide
> a new sewer, but only that they have neglected to
> clear out an existing sewer, and so have caused a
> nuisance to the plaintiffs. I cannot see why the
> defendants should not be subject to an action to
> compel them to use their sewer in a reasonable
> manner. The first part of section 299 of the 1875

---

[1] Section 19 thereof.
[2] *Stretton's Derby Brewery Co. v. Derby Corporation* [1894] 1 Ch. 431;
but in *Brown v. Sargent* (1858), 1 F. & F. 112, it had been said, *per* Erle,
J., that negligence would be negatived if the true cause of the nuisance was
natural, and could not reasonably have been anticipated.
[3] Under, *e.g.*, s. 13 of the 1875 Act.
[4] *R. v. Epsom Guardians* (1863), 27 J.P. 4868.
[5] (1900), 63 L.T. 363; Lord Halsbury is giving judgment in the Court of
Appeal.

Act [which corresponded in this respect to section 322 of the 1936 Act] refers to the construction of new sewage works, and the only difficulty here can arise from the subsequent words of the section as to maintaining existing sewers. I agree with the learned judge [in the court below] that the maintenance of a sewer is not the same thing as that which it is the duty of the local authority to do by virtue of section 19 [of the 1875 Act], that is, to keep the sewer so that it shall not be a nuisance or injurious to health, and to see that it is properly cleansed. Section 299 does not, in my opinion, touch the duty of the local authority to use proper diligence in the ordinary course of the management of their sewers, and I cannot see anything in the section to show that a private person who has suffered damages by the neglect of such a duty by the local authority may not have a right of action in consequence."

It is not altogether clear how far this principle applies at the present time, as complaint may be made to the Secretary of State under section 322 of the 1936 Act in respect of a failure to discharge **any** of the functions of a water authority or a local authority under the Act of 1936 as amended. It is submitted however, that wherever an authority have been guilty of some act,[1] which amounts to a breach of a duty under the statute, and whereby a nuisance has been occasioned to the damage of the plaintiff, an action will lie at the suit of the person aggrieved. This must follow, it seems, as a

---

[1] And have not merely "inherited" drains or sewers under the Public Health Acts, which constitute a nuisance by reason only that they have ceased to deal adequately with the sewage of the authority's district; *see per* Evershed, M.R., in *Pride of Derby v. British Celanese*, [1953] 1 All E.R. 179, at p. 194.

consequence of section 31 of the 1936 Act, and has been recognised in several cases.[1]

The second general duty of water authorities with regard to the subject matter of this Chapter, is, subject to certain safeguards considered later,[2] to accept into their public sewers foul water and surface water from premises entitled to drain into such sewers.[3]

2. THE RECOVERY OF EXPENSES.

In certain limited circumstances, the water authority may be entitled to recover the expenses incurred by them in maintaining a particular length of a public sewer vested in them, from those private individuals who (generally speaking) would have been liable for the maintenance of that length of sewer under the law in force prior to the Act of 1936.[4] This right of recovery[5] is exercisable only in the circumstances mentioned below, and in any proceedings under the section, the water authority must be prepared to prove that all these matters apply to the particular case before the court.

(a) Work of maintenance only.

Expenses are recoverable only in respect of work of maintenance on the particular length of sewer in question. The ordinary meaning of the word "maintenance" is expanded for the purposes of the section to include[6]

---

[1] *Haigh v. Deudraeth R.D.C.*, [1945] 2 All E.R. 661, and *Pride of Derby v. British Celanese (supra)*. If flooding is caused by overloading of sewers which arose not from any act of the authority, but because they were obliged to accept sewage from new development into their sewer under s. 34 of the 1936 Act, the authority are not liable: *Smeaton v. Ilford Corporation*, [1954] 1 All E.R. 923.

[2] *Post*, p. 81.

[3] 1936 Act, s. 34, and *post*, Chap. 9, p. 118.

[4] 1936 Act, s. 24.

[5] It is a power, not a duty, and is therefore not enforceable at the instance of a ratepayer, against the authority.

[6] Not to "mean."

"repair, renewal and improvement",[1] but no mention is made of "cleansing".[2] It is submitted, although the point has not been before the superior courts, that cleansing is **not** here included in "maintenance", and that, therefore, expenses incurred by a water authority (or by a local authority pursuant to arrangements with the water authority made under s. 15 of the Water Act 1973) on work of cleansing only are not recoverable under the section. "Repair, renewal and improvement" are all operations necessitating some constructional work, which is not necessary in cleansing, and "maintain" in its ordinary meaning (normally in relation to buildings or structures) involves the idea of keeping in good repair; moreover, it is arguable that, by mentioning both "maintain" and "cleanse" in section 23, the legislature understood the two terms as being mutually exclusive and that this distinction should be drawn in the present section also. The cost, therefore, of the clearance of obstructions, would seem not to be recoverable under the section.

"Improvement" for the purposes of this section, includes only such improvement as may be necessary to make the particular length of sewer "adequate for draining the premises served by it immediately before the improvement was undertaken".[3] If the authority otherwise improve or enlarge the length of sewer so that it may serve additional premises, their expenses in so doing will be recoverable only in so far as the works were necessary for draining the premises originally served thereby; and on such enlargement, etc., the particular length of sewer ceases to be one to which the section applies (*see* section 24 (2)).

---

[1] 1936 Act, s. 24 (1).
[2] Compare s. 23, *ante*, p. 66.
[3] 1936 Act, s. 24 (1).

(b) Length to which the section applies.

In order that the right of recovery given by the section may operate, the length of sewer in respect of which the authority's expenses have been incurred, must be one to which the section applies.

The section applies to two different types of "lengths", both of which must have been constructed before 1st October, 1937, as detailed below.

Sub. Para. (a) of s. 24 (4).

"A length for the maintenance of which persons other than the local authority were, immediately before the commencement of this Act,[1] responsible by virtue either of some enactment or statutory scheme relating to combined drains or of an order made under such an enactment or scheme, or of an agreement, being an enactment, scheme, order or agreement whereby the authority were entitled to require those persons to maintain that length of the sewer, or to abate any nuisance therein, or to contribute in proportions to, or indemnify the authority against, any expenses incurred by the authority in maintaining it."[2]

Liability to bear the cost of maintenance of such a "length" accrued under the pre-1937 law in the following circumstances:

A.—*Under statute.*

The commonest example of liability attaching under an enactment was in respect of a length of sewer that was a "single private drain", within the meaning of section 19 of the Public Health Acts Amendment Act,

---

[1] 1st October, 1937. *See* s. 347 (1) of the Act, and Water Act 1973, Schedule 8, para. 34. References in this sub-section to "the local authority" are to be read as referring to the responsible local authority in 1974.

[2] 1936 Act, s. 24 (4) (*a*).

1890,[1] or the many local Acts drafted in similar, but wider terms.[2] This section of the 1890 Act has been set out and discussed in an earlier Chapter,[3] but it is here necessary to list the essential features of a particular conduit to entitle it to the status of a "single private drain". These are as follows:

(1) The conduit in question must serve more than one house,[4] two at least of which are[5] in separate ownerships[6];

(2) A particular conduit does not commence to be a single private drain until at least two houses, separately owned, are drained thereby[7];

(3) The system of drainage in question must be

---

[1] In those sanitary districts where the Act had been adopted before the repeal of this section by the 1936 Act.
[2] The usual form of these local Act sections was to remove the requirement of the 1890 Act that the drain should serve at least two houses in **separate** ownership.
[3] *See* Chap. 2, *ante*, p. 20.
[4] Note that the term used is "house", not "building".
[5] The present tense is used in this paragraph, although regard should be had to the position as it was immediately prior to the coming into operation of the 1936 Act.
[6] In *Bradford v. Eastbourne Corporation*, [1896] 2 Q.B. 205, all the houses served by the drain were owned by different owners; in *Thompson v. Eccles Corporation*, [1905] 1 K.B. 110, some of the houses belonged to one owner, but others belonged to other persons. In *Wood Green U.D.C. v. Joseph*, [1908] A.C. 419, which (although it was a decision of the House of Lords) has been considered in subsequent cases to be a most unsatisfactory case, the houses (some of which were owned by different persons) were drained in pairs, each common pipe from a pair of houses draining into the conduit in question. As the system of drainage had not been required to be provided by the local authority under s. 23 or s. 25 of the 1875 Act, the Law Lords (and Lord Atkinson in particular) held that the conduit was **not** a single private drain. This particular point was not clearly raised in the previous decisions (although in *Kingston-upon-Hull Corporation v. N.E.R. Co.*, [1915] 1 Ch. 456, the s. 23 notice was produced in Court), and the reasoning behind the House of Lords' decision in the instant case is not readily appreciated.
[7] *Jackson v. Wimbledon U.D.C.*, [1905] 2 K.B. 27.

one which was required by the local authority under section 23 or section 25 of the 1875 Act[1];

(4) The drain must be "private"; *i.e.*, it must have been laid in private land, and constructed (before 1937) by some person other than the local authority or their predecessors in title. Private land is here widely understood, for a conduit laid through the sub-soil of a street repairable by the inhabitants at large, was none the less held to be capable of being a "single private drain", for the sub-soil remained the property of the frontages to the street[2];

(5) The conduit in question must drain into a public sewer,[3] and not merely into a cesspool.[4] It is apparently not even sufficient if it drains to the sea.

B.—*Under a statutory scheme.*

The commonest example of liability under the section attaching pursuant to a statutory scheme[5] was liability under a town planning scheme made under the Town and Country Planning Act, 1932.[6]

C.—*Under an agreement.*

Agreements for the combined drainage of premises were frequently entered into under the 1875 Act,

---

[1] *Wood Green U.D.C. v. Joseph* (*supra*); followed and applied with some reluctance in *Hill v. Aldershot Corporation*, [1933] 1 K.B. 259. These sections empowered the local authority to compel an existing house that was "without a drain sufficient for effectual drainage", to be adequately drained, and also prohibited the building or re-building of a house unless and until an effectual drain had been provided therefor.

[2] *Kingston-upon-Hull Corporation v. N.E.R. Co.* (*supra*).

[3] *See* the wording of the section. This requirement in itself causes difficulty, as a single private drain may be none the less a public sewer (*see* Chap. 2, *ante*, p. 21). Presumably this portion of the section must be construed as referring to a public sewer which is not itself a single private drain.

[4] *Cf.* Chap. 1, *ante*, p. 5, and *Butt v. Snow* (1903), 89 L.T. 302.

[5] *I.e.*, a scheme made under any enactment: 1936 Act, s. 343 (1).

[6] *See* Chap. 2, *ante*, p. 22.

whereby the local authority approved such a proposal, subject to the owner agreeing to keep the combined drain in repair at his expense. Such an agreement was enforceable, however, only against the original party thereto, and it was this factor and the consequent unfortunate consequences to the local authority, that seems to have been the genesis of section 19 of the Public Health Acts Amendment Act, 1890.[1]

Sub-Para. (b) of s. 24 (4).

"A length which was vested in the local authority immediately before the commencement of this Act,[2] but was not constructed at their expense or at the expense of any authority whose successors they are, and which lies in a garden, court or yard belonging to any of the premises served by the sewer or common to any two or more of them, or lies under a building comprised in any of those premises, or lies in a roadway, footway, passage or alley which is used solely or mainly as a means of access to those premises or any of them, but is not a highway repairable by the inhabitants at large."[3]

This is an alternative to (i), above, and in some circumstances it may be easier to bring a particular length of sewer within the provisions of sub-paragraph (ii), than within sub-paragraph (i), where the amount of "ancient history" that must be proved by the plaintiff local authority (in proceedings for the recovery of expenses under the section) may be too great in the particular case. On the other hand, sub-paragraph (ii) will normally be of narrower application than sub-paragraph (i)—for example, a conduit laid under a high-

---

[1] *Butt v. Snow* (1903), 89 L.T. 302. As such agreements did not bind successive owners, they were not registrable in the local land charges register (after 1925).
[2] 1st October, 1937; and *see* Water Act 1973, Schedule 8, para. 34.
[3] 1936 Act, s. 24 (4) (*b*); and *see* now Highways Act, 1980, s. 36.

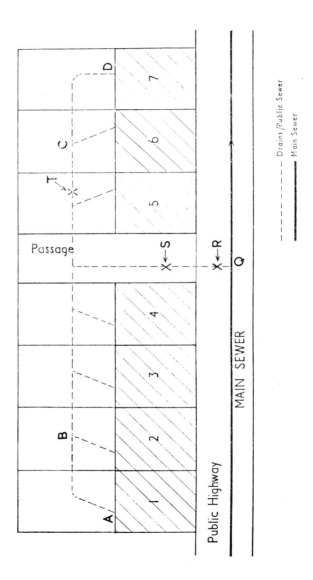

way maintainable at the public expense is none the less capable of being a "single private drain".[1]

Thus, in the diagram on the preceding page, the entire lengths A-Q and D-Q are private drains, but only the lengths B-Q and C-Q (where the drainage of more than one premises is taken) are single private drains; if they were constructed prior to 1st October, 1937, they are public sewers, vested in the water authority by virtue of s. 20 of the 1936 Act (as amended). Lengths B-Q and C-Q are also lengths to which s. 24 applies provided the requirements set out on p. 73, *supra*, are satisfied and therefore a defect at point R when "maintained" (*i.e.* rectified) by the water authority would give rise to liability to pay the expenses incurred, by the owners of premises 1-7 (presumably in equal proportions). However, if the requirements applicable to s. 24 (4) (*a*) cannot all be met, expenses in this case cannot be recovered under s. 24 (4) (*b*), as the point R is within a highway repairable at the public expense. If the defect occurs at point S para. (*b*) **will** apply, and there is no need to prove the facts establishing a case under para. (*a*). If the defect occurs at point T, the owners of houses 6 and 7 only would be liable (under para. (*a*) **or** (*b*)).

(c) Service of notices.

Proceedings may be brought under the section (except as hereinafter mentioned) only if the appropriate notices have been served. By virtue of the proviso to section 24 (1), notice[2] of the work the authority propose to undertake must be given to the owners of any premises known to them to be served by the length of sewer in question, at least seven days before the commence-

---

[1] *Kingston-upon-Hull Corporation v. N.E.R. Co.*, [1916] 1 Ch. 31.

[2] This must be in writing and signed by the appropriate authorised officer of the authority (s. 284 of the 1936 Act), and must be served in the prescribed manner (s. 285, *ibid.*). It need not be in any particular form, but Shaw's Form PN 9 is appropriate.

ment of the work. The authority must also consider "any representations as to the need for, and reasonableness of, the proposed work which may be made to them by any of those owners within seven days of the service of the notice". There is no need, however, for the service of any notices at all if the water authority considers immediate action is necessary.[1]

A local authority can delegate any of their functions to one of their officers by virtue of s. 101 of the Local Government Act, 1972, but this does not seem to apply to water authorities.[2]

General Observations.

The authority having satisfied the above requirements, they may recover their expenses reasonably incurred from the owners for the time being of the various premises served by the particular length of sewer, in such proportions as they "think it fair to fix".[3] In so apportioning the expenses, the authority must have regard to all the circumstances of the case, and in particular, "the benefit derived by each owner from that length of sewer, the distance for which it is laid in land belonging to each owner, the point at which any work was necessary, and the responsibility for any act or default which rendered the work necessary".[4] In a case such as that shown on the diagram on page 76, the apportionment will normally be made equally between the seven premises served by the length of sewer (note that houses 1 and 7, although served directly by drains, and not by the public sewer, should not be omitted from the apportionment). The authority

---

[1] P.H.A., 1936, s. 24 (1); s. 15 of the Public Health Act 1961 amending this subsection has been repealed by the Water Act, 1973, Schedule 9.
[2] Unless the very wide powers of Schedule 3, para. 2, of the 1973 Act, can be construed to cover this point.
[3] 1936 Act, s. 24 (1).
[4] *Ibid.*

should serve a demand[1] for payment of these apportioned expenses, and they thereupon become a charge on the premises.[2] Recovery may be by way of summary proceedings under section 58 of the Magistrates' Courts Act, 1980, or as for a simple contract debt in any court of competent jurisdiction,[3] which will normally be the county court. The authority are entitled by order to declare the expenses payable by instalments,[4] and they are also entitled to include in the expenses recoverable as above, a reasonable sum by way of establishment charges.[5]

The legality of the action taken by the authority, and the recoverability of their expenses will, of course, be matters which the court will be entitled to take into consideration in proceedings brought by them to recover such expenses; and, the onus of proving that the section applies rests on the authority. On the other hand, any owner affected may, if he so chooses,[6] apply to the local magistrates' court, and they may then determine any question "as to whether any length of sewer is one to which this section applies, as to the necessity for any work carried out by a water authority, as to the amount, or the reasonableness, of the expenses incurred by them, or as to the fairness of any division or apportionment of expenses made by them".[7]

---

[1] This must be duly signed and served (*see* note [2], on p. 77), but need not be in any particular form.

[2] 1936 Act, s. 291 (1). Although this charge is acquired by a water authority (or possibly by a new town development corporation under s. 34 of the New Towns Act 1965), it is registrable in the local land charges register, under s. 1 (1) (a) of the Local Land Charges Act 1975, which came into force on 1.8.77.

[3] 1936 Act, s. 293; and *see Great Yarmouth Corporation v. Gibson*, [1956] 1 Q.B. 573, and Chap. 11, *post*, p. 177.

[4] 1936 Act, s. 291 (2).

[5] Local Government Act 1974, s. 36; applied by Water Act, 1973, s. 14 (2).

[6] There will not be much advantage to be gained by taking such proceedings; in most circumstances an owner concerned would be best advised to await proceedings being commenced against him by the local authority for the recovery of expenses.

[7] 1936 Act, s. 24 (3).

Appeals.

An appeal lies from a decision of the magistrates to the Crown court on proceedings brought by the water authority,[1] or on an application by an owner,[2] and such appeal may be based on either questions of law or of fact; alternatively either party may appeal by way of case stated on a point of law to the Queen's Bench Division,[3] and if the magistrates refuse to state a case, they may be compelled to do so (in a proper case) by *mandamus* proceedings.[4] Appeal lies from the decision of the county court (or the High Court),[5] to the Court of Appeal on a point of law.[6]

3.   THE ALTERATION AND CLOSURE, ETC., OF PUBLIC SEWERS.

The water authority are expressly empowered[7] to alter the size of course of any public sewer, either entirely, or for the purpose only of foul water or only of surface water drainage. If it were not for this provision, it seems that, although the sewer were vested in the authority, they would have no power to stop it up,[8] their property rights in the sewer being vested in them subject to the duty to use the same for the drainage of their area. Even under the present section, the authority, before exercising these powers, may not deprive any person of the use of a sewer for any purpose

---

[1] 1936 Act, s. 301; provided that in the particular case the water authority are a "person aggrieved": *see* Chap. 11, *post*, p. 179.

[2] Under s. 24 (3), *supra*; the appeal lies under s. 301 of the Act.

[3] Administration of Justice (Miscellaneous Provisions) Act, 1938, s. 19.

[4] *Ibid.*; The Crown court cannot be so compelled: *R. v. Somerset Justices, ex p. Cole*, [1950] 1 All E.R. 264.

[5] The High Court alone will have jurisdiction in debt (*see* s. 293 of the 1936 Act) where the amount involved exceeds £750—*see* County Courts Act, 1959, s. 39 (as amended by the Administration of Justice Act, 1969, s. 1).

[6] As of right, where the amount claimed exceeds £20: County Courts Act, 1959, s. 108.

[7] *See* s. 22 of the 1936 Act; this is a power, not a duty.

[8] *Attorney-General v. Dorking Union* (1882), 20 Ch. D. 595; *Attorney-General v. Acton Local Board* (1882), 22 Ch. D. 221, and *ante*, Chap. 2, pp. 12 and 15.

for which he is lawfully using it, without first providing a "sewer equally effective for his use for that purpose", and they must also bear the expense of any work necessary to make his drains or sewers communicate with the sewer so provided.[1]

It is not an offence to continue to use a sewer which has been stopped up under this provision, or even one the use of which has been prohibited,[2] but the natural result of ignoring such action taken by the authority would normally be to cause a nuisance,[3] and the local authority will then be able to take abatement proceedings against the person responsible under sections 92–100 of the 1936 Act.

In exercising their powers under this[4] section, the water authority may not create a nuisance; another reason compelling the authority to provide a substitute before closing a sewer.[5] It should, moreover, be noted that where an authority have vested in them a sewer constructed by private persons, which lies in or under a private street not adopted by the local authority, they may still use section 22 of the 1936 Act; but they cannot use the powers of the private street works code,[6] to recover the cost of such alterations from the frontagers to the street.[7]

Special statutory powers exist for the alteration of

---

[1] 1936 Act, s. 22.

[2] There is no right to drain foul water into a surface water sewer, and *vice versa; see* s. 34 of the 1936 Act, and *post*, p. 119. If such prohibition were disregarded, the local authority could apply for an injunction.

[3] Whereas the authority have a discretion whether or not to exercise their powers under s. 22, it would seem that they might be liable to disallowance by the District Auditor if they had expended money under the section without good and sufficient reasons.

[4] And other sections in Part II of the Act; *see ante*, p. 72.

[5] An injunction could be obtained to stop the authority from causing a nuisance: *R. v. Bradford Navigation Co.* (1865), 29 J.P. 613.

[6] *See* Part XI of the Highways Act, 1980.

[7] *Fulham District Board of Works v. Goodwin* (1876), 1 Ex. D. 400; *Bonella v. Twickenham Local Board* (1888), 20 Q.B.D. 63; but *see* p. 45, *ante*.

public sewers by the British Gas Corporation (Gas Act, 1972, Schedule 4, para. 1), an Electricity Board (clause 18 in the Schedule to the Electric Lighting (Clauses) Act, 1899, and Electricity Act, 1947), tramway undertakers (Tramways Act, 1870, section 31), and water authorities acting as water supply undertakers (clauses 22 and 70 in the Third Schedule to the Water Act, 1945), but if these powers are exceeded in any particular case, the undertakers will be liable in nuisance to the water authority. Cemetery companies may not cause their sewers or drains to connect with public sewers, except with the consent of the water authority.[1]

4.   THE PRESERVATION OF PUBLIC SEWERS.

One method by which the water authority are entitled to preserve their public sewers, is to regulate the use thereof by persons draining their premises into such sewers; this subject is discussed later in this Chapter.[2] More positive powers are, however, also vested in the authority for this purpose.

(a) Buildings over Sewers.

In general, no new building may be erected over any sewer or drain shown on the local authority's sewer map,[3] without their consent. This control, contained in section 25 of the 1936 Act, is made effective through the medium of the Building Regulations, 1976,[4] as the local authority are required by this section to reject any plans for the erection of a building or of an exten-

---

[1] Cemetery Clauses Act, 1847, s. 18, applied by the effect of s. 14 (2) of the Water Act, 1973.

[2] *See* para. 5, *post*, p. 88.

[3] Required to be maintained under s. 32 of the 1936 Act; *see* Chap. 3, *ante*, p. 48.

[4] Made by the Secretary of State under the P.H.A., 1961. The section therefore applies only to buildings for which plans must be submitted under the Regulations; and *see* note [1] on p. 85. This control formerly applied to building byelaws, but byelaws were replaced by the Regulations in February 1966.

sion to a building, submitted under the Regulations,[1] which show such a building, etc., as being proposed to be erected over any such drain or sewer unless they are satisfied that in the circumstances of the particular case they may "properly" consent to the erection of the proposed building or extension. Moreover, in exercising this discretion, the local authority must notify the water authority of the proposal, and the water authority then may give the local authority directions as to the manner in which they are to exercise their functions.[2] Any work constructed in contravention of the Regulations (*e.g.*, without submission of plans, or otherwise than in accordance with the deposited plans) may be removed by the authority at the building owner's expense,[3] and such construction will normally constitute an offence under the Regulations.[4]

If any building had been erected before 1st October, 1937, over a sewer without such consent of the local authority as was required under section 26 of the 1875 Act,[5] the authority may by notice require the building owner to pull it down or to alter it as necessary, and, in default of compliance with such requirement, the authority may act themselves and recover their expenses thereby incurred from the person in default.[6]

"Building" is not defined generally for the purposes of the 1936 Act, but it is normally understood as signifying any construction or erection capable of enclos-

---

[1] As to the Building Regulations generally, *see* Chap. 9, *post*, p. 126.

[2] Water Act 1973, s. 14 (6) and (7).

[3] Provided the work is in actual contravention of the Act or the Regulations and also provided the appropriate procedure is observed; *see* s. 65 of the 1936 Act, as amended by the 1961 Act.

[4] P.H.A., 1961, s. 4 (6).

[5] This section was not in force in all rural districts.

[6] 1936 Act, s. 25 (3). In *Ilford U.D.C. v. Beal*, [1925] 1 K.B. 671, it was held that a building owner was not responsible for damage to a sewer under his property of which he was unaware (and in circumstances in which it could not have been said that he ought reasonably to have been aware of its existence), but it seems that this argument would not provide a defence to proceedings taken under the present section.

ing some area of ground.[1] In the present context, however, the purpose of the section is clearly to prevent damage to sewers, and to provide the water authority with ready access thereto, and it has therefore been suggested that "a building to be within the section must be one which, by reason of its weight or otherwise, may cause an injury to the sewer over which it has been built, or one which, by reason of its size or otherwise, prevents access being gained to the sewer".[2]

(b) Injuries to Sewers.

In addition to the express safeguard contained in section 25 of the 1936 Act, a water authority have sufficient ownership in a public sewer[3] to entitle them to bring an action in nuisance for damages or an injunction in a case of injury to their sewers.[4] In actual

---

[1] *See, e.g.*, the suggestion in *Slaughter v. Sunderland Corporation* (1891), 60 L.J. M.C. 91. The roofing over of an open space between walls or buildings is deemed to be the erection of a building for the present purpose; 1936 Act, s. 90 (2) (ii).

[2] *Urban Housing Co., Ltd. v. City of Oxford*, [1939] 3 All E.R. 839, *per* Bennett, J., at p. 850, where he suggested that two walls, each 7 feet high and 9 inches thick, were not buildings within the meaning of s. 26 of the 1875 Act (the predecessor of the present section). Sir Wilfrid Greene, M.R., however, in giving the judgment of the Court of Appeal in the same case ([1939] 4 All E.R. 211, at p. 221, upholding the judgment of Bennett, J.), said that he would have been disposed to take the view that these walls were buildings within the section, as "there must be, on the face of it, some slight interference, or might be some slight interference, owing to their presence, with the facility of repairing or re-laying the sewers". Both the observation here referred to were, however, *obiter*. It should also be noted that in one respect the 1936 Act section is narrower in its operation than its predecessor in the 1875 Act, which was under consideration in this case. The section now in force relates only to buildings or extensions of buildings the erection of which necessitates the submission of plans under the Regulations; the 1875 Act section was a straight prohibition against causing any building to be "newly erected over any sewer of the urban authority", without the authority's written consent.

[3] But *see* Chap. 2, *ante*, p. 12.

[4] *See, e.g., Cleckheaton U.D.C. v. Firth* (1898), 62 J.P. 536, although in that case it was held that the defendant was legally entitled to do the act complained of. In *Gas Light and Coke Co. v. St. Mary Abbotts Kensington, Vestry* (1885), 15 Q.B.D. 1, an injunction was granted to prevent the highway authority from using a heavy steam roller for road repairs in such a manner as would injure gas mains laid in the highway at a depth and protected sufficiently against all ordinary traffic, and in *Driscoll v. Poplar Board of Works* (1897), 62 J.P. 40, the same principle was applied in an action for damages.

practice, however, it may more commonly be convenient for the local authority to take proceedings as for a public nuisance against the person responsible,[1] as most injuries to public sewers will result in such a nuisance.[2]

Such action, which by s. 92 of the 1936 Act it would be the duty of the local authority to take, does not of course involve the water authority. Clearly the two authorities should act in close co-operation, but if the water authority feel they are compelled to act themselves, it seems that they would be confined to non-statutory remedies, exercisable by virtue of their ownership of the sewer in question.

(c) Support of Sewers: removal of minerals.

The Public Health Act, 1875 (Support of Sewers) Amendment Act, 1883, regulates the rights of a water authority to subjacent support of any "sanitary work"[3] vested in them or under their control. The owners of the subsoil may not prejudice such support by the removal of minerals other than coal, etc., by the National Coal Board (*see* below, para. (**d**)) without first giving notice[4] to the authority, who may then within 30 days[5] require the minerals to be left unworked, in which case

---

[1] If the person responsible cannot be found, the owner of the sewer or drain in question will be liable in proceedings under the "nuisance clauses": *Rhymney Iron Co. v. Gelligaer U.D.C.*, [1917] 1 K.B. 589.

[2] *See, e.g., Riddell v. Spear* (1879), 40 L.T. 130.

[3] This expression is defined in s. 2 of the Act, and includes a great many other things besides sewers (in spite of the title of the Act), such as water pipes, street lighting, etc. It seems that the Act applies to water authorities in respect of their sewerage functions by virtue of the closing words of s. 14 (2) of the Water Act 1973.

[4] Of their intention to work the minerals. This notice may relate to a considerable area of land: *Bolsover U.D.C. v. Bolsover Colliery Co.*, [1947] 1 All E.R. 130.

[5] *See* s. 3, incorporating ss. 18 to 28 of the Waterworks Clauses Act, 1847; they may give notice to prevent or interfere with the working of the mines in question. The 1847 Act has been repealed by the Water Act, 1945, but this repeal does not affect the present Act; *Maxwell on Interpretation of Statutes*, 11th edn., p. 389.

The rights of the National Coal Board are subject to this statute: Coal Act, 1938, s. 34 (1); Coal Industry Nationalisation Act, 1946, s. 5.

the authority must pay compensation for such minerals[1]; alternatively, the authority may specify and define a limited nature and extent of support which they require to be left.[2] If the authority take no action on the notice from the landowner, the latter may then work his minerals, but he will still, apparently, be liable to the authority in respect of any damage occasioned to their sewers if he works the mines otherwise than in "a reasonable and proper manner".[3] Unless the authority serve a notice to treat for the mining rights or for a limited right of support as above mentioned, they are not compelled to pay any compensation to the owners of the subsoil.

The special rights afforded by this Act are limited in two respects:

(a) They apply only to support removed as a consequence of **mining operations** (other than coal: *see below*). In other cases the landowner through whose land a public sewer is laid is under a statutory obligation (by virtue of the powers given to the authority by the Public Health Acts to maintain the sewer) to provide subjacent support to such sewer, and compensation must be paid to him by the authority if he can prove he has suffered any loss as a consequence thereof.[4] It seems that, apart from this right based on statute, the local authority has no natural right of support for its sewers.[5]

(b) **The procedure** of the Act, and of the Water-

---

[1] This will be assessed in accordance with the Land Compensation Act, 1961; in case of dispute, by the Lands Tribunal (Lands Tribunal Act, 1949).

[2] Act of 1883, s. 3 (2). The amount of support required to be left may be more or less than 40 yards; the authority not being restricted to this distance under the 1883 Act, as was the case with undertakers under the 1847 Act.

[3] This appears to follow from s. 4 of the 1883 Act.

[4] *Re Dudley Corporation* (1881), 8 Q.B.D. 86.

[5] *Newcastle Corporation v. Wolstanton Ltd.*, [1947] 1 All E.R. 218.

works Clauses Act, 1847, incorporated therewith, **must have been observed**; in particular, the authority must have made and deposited maps showing the course of their sewers.[1]

Where the sewer had been constructed prior to the passing of the 1883 Act,[2] and a right of support had been acquired in respect thereof, the procedure of the Act does not apply in respect thereto, provided that the authority can prove that no compensation was recoverable in respect of such right of support under the law in force prior to the passing of the Act.[3]

(d) Support of Sewers: removal of coal, etc.

Where the National Coal Board (in whom all coal and strata of coal is now vested[4]) withdraw support from land in connection with the lawful working and getting of coal, or of coal and other minerals worked therewith, and thereby cause damage to a public sewer, the

---

[1] Under ss. 19-21 of the Waterworks Clauses Act, 1847, as applied by s. 3 of the Act of 1883. These maps must be to a scale of not less than one foot to a mile, and must be deposited with the proper officer of the county council and with the "clerks of the several parishes in England", in which such works are situate. It is possible that these maps are not required for works which are above ground only: *per* Roxburgh, J., in *Bolsover U.D.C. v. Bolsover Colliery*, [1947] 1 All E.R. 130, at p. 133.

[2] 25th August, 1883.

[3] In *Newcastle Corporation v. Wolstanton Ltd.* (*supra*), the plaintiff local authority failed to establish any claim against the defendant mining company in respect of the letting down of land through mining operations whereby the authority's gas mains had been injured. The 1883 Act could not be invoked as the authority had not prepared and deposited the necessary maps, but as the Act had been passed, the authority could not claim the implied right of support given by the re *Dudley Corporation* (*supra*) principle, which was expressly excluded from mining cases by the 1883 Act (by s. 4 thereof). On the other hand, the principle stated in the text, contained in s. 5 of the 1883 Act, also could not be invoked in respect of those mains which were in existence prior to the passing of the Act, as the authority could not prove the absence of any right to compensation under the pre-1883 law. For a case where the absence of any such right to compensation could be proved, and to which therefore, s. 5 of the 1883 Act applied, *see Jary v. Barnsley Corporation*, [1907] 2 Ch. 600.

[4] Coal Industry Nationalisation Act. 1946.

Board will be liable to make a payment in respect of such subsidence damage to the water authority in whom such sewer is vested, in accordance with the provisions of the Coal-Mining (Subsidence) Act, 1957.[1]

5. THE USE OF PUBLIC SEWERS.

The rights of a private person to cause the drains of his premises to be connected to a public sewer vested in a water authority are discussed later,[2] but it is here necessary briefly to mention the statutory provisions which restrict the liquids and substances that may be permitted to flow into a public sewer. These provisions may be considered as follows:

(a) Certain matters not to be passed into public sewers.
This is the wording of the side-note to section 27 of the 1936 Act, which makes it a criminal offence (proceedings for which may be taken at the instance of the water authority[3]) to "throw, empty or turn, or suffer or permit to be thrown or emptied or to pass, into any public sewer, or into any drain or sewer communicating with a public sewer", any of the following:

" (i) any matter likely to injure the sewer or drain or to interfere with the free flow of its contents, or to affect prejudicially the treatment and disposal of its contents[4]; **or**

(ii) any chemical refuse or waste steam, or any liquid of a temperature higher than 110 de-

---

[1] In most cases a "damage notice" must be served under s. 2 (1) of the Act in accordance with the Coal-Mining (Subsidence) (Damage Notice) Regulations, 1957, S.I. 1957, No. 1405.
[2] See Chap. 9, post, p. 118.
[3] P.H.A. 1936, s. 298, applied by s. 14 (2) of the Water Act, 1973.
[4] See Liverpool Corporation v. Coghill (H.) & Son, Ltd., [1918] 1 Ch. 307, where the particular effluent had a deleterious effect on the land on which the sewage matter was eventually deposited. In this case also it was suggested obiter, by Eve, J., that a local authority could not grant a right to a person to cause effluent to flow into public sewers in such a manner as to cause a nuisance.

grees Fahrenheit, being refuse or steam which, or a liquid which when so heated, is, either alone or in combination with the contents of the sewer or drain, dangerous, or the cause of a nuisance, or prejudicial to health[1]; **or**

(iii) any petroleum spirit,[2] or carbide of calcium."

(b) Trade Effluent.

Under the Public Health (Drainage of Trade Premises) Act, 1937, which is discussed in more detail later,[3] no trade effluent[4] (unless it is of a type which may lawfully be discharged into a public sewer[5]) may be discharged from trade premises[6] into a public sewer otherwise than in accordance with a written notice given to the water authority.[7]

(c) Common Law.

In addition to the above statutory provisions, the water authority may sue for damages or an injunction if it can be shown that an injury is being caused to a public sewer vested in them as a consequence of any effluent, etc., being permitted to flow into the sewer,

---

[1] *See* para. (c) below.

[2] Defined in s. 27 (3) as meaning "any such (*a*) crude petroleum; (*b*) oil made from petroleum, or from coal, shale, peat or other bituminous substances; or (*c*) product of petroleum or mixture containing petroleum, as, when tested in the manner prescribed by or under the Petroleum (Consolidation) Act, 1928, gives off an inflammable vapour at a temperature of less than 73 degrees Fahrenheit". In addition to the above control, it is customary to insert in a licence to store petroleum spirit under s. 1 of the Petroleum (Consolidation) Act, 1928 (which licence is issued by the county council; Local Government Act 1972, Sched. 29, para. 32), a condition to the effect that no spirit or vapour shall be allowed to escape into any drain or sewer.

[3] *See* Chap. 9, *post*, p. 145.

[4] Defined in s. 14 (1) of the 1937 Act; *post*, p. 145.

[5] Under s. 1 of the 1937 Act.

[6] "Any premises used or intended to be used for carrying on any trade or industry": 1937 Act, s. 14 (1).

[7] 1937 Act, s. 2.

unless the person responsible has a prescriptive right therefor. Moreover, if the injury is sufficiently serious, proceedings may be brought by the local authority for a public nuisance under the "nuisance clauses" of the 1936 Act.[1] Normally, the remedy afforded by section 27 of the Act will be adequate, but it seems that the courts would grant an injunction to prevent any contravention of that section in a proper case where the penalties of the section can be shown to be inadequate.[2]

---

[1] For an example where such proceedings were successful, *see St. Helens Chemical Co. v. St. Helens Corporation* (1876), 1 Ex. D. 196.

[2] Lumley's "Public Health", 12th edn., Vol. III, p. 2292. Also *see Att.-Gen. v. Sharp*, [1931] 1 Ch. 121, and *Att.-Gen. v. Bastow*, [1957] 1 Q.B. 514.

CHAPTER 6

HIGHWAY DRAINS

1. HIGHWAY DRAINS AS PUBLIC SEWERS.

In this Chapter the expression "highway drain" is used as meaning any conduit or ditch (artificial or natural) which takes off or conveys the surface water from a highway[1] maintainable at the public expense.[2] There is no significance, in this context, in distinguishing between a drain and a sewer, as there are no lega consequences of any such distinction.

The drains which take off the surface water from a highway—which "belong" to the highway in question[3]— and which serve no other purpose will normally be vested in the highway authority[4] as such, and there will in most cases be no question of them being vested in the water authority as public sewers under section 20 of the Act of 1936. Where, however, a highway drain also conveys foul or surface water from premises in the vicinity of the highway, or where it is desired to connect the drains of such premises to a highway drain, the status of the latter may well be very important; in particular it will have to be ascertained whether or not the drain is a public sewer.

---

[1] This term is used in its widest sense as comprising "all portions of land over which every subject of the Crown may lawfully pass" (Pratt and Mackenzie's *Law of Highways*, 21st edn., p. 1).
[2] Private streets are considered below, p. 98.
[3] The expression used in s. 266 (1) of the Highways Act, 1980.
[4] By s. 265 of the Highways Act, 1980, every highway maintainable at the public expense vests in the highway authority. All such highways are now vested in the county councils, under ss. 1 and 265 of the 1980 Act, although urban roads, footpaths and bridleways may be maintained by the district council. The only exceptions are trunk and special roads, vested in the Secretary of State (1980 Act, s. 1).

Highway drains constructed subsequent to 1st October, 1937, by the highway authority, will be public sewers if they have been constructed under some statutory provision relating to the sewering of private streets[1]; they will also be public sewers if they were constructed before 1st April 1974 by a highway authority who were at that time also the local sanitary authority and provided they then drained other property not belonging to the local authority.[2]

If such drains drained the highway alone, or if they were constructed by a highway authority (before or after 1st April 1974) who were not the local sanitary authority, they will not be public sewers, unless and until the water authority have made a declaration of vesting,[3] on the application of the highway authority.[4] On the other hand a statute transferring liability for a highway from one local authority to another only affected "functions with respect to highways", and therefore did not transfer responsibility for a land drain to the new highway authority.[5]

A highway drain constructed prior to 1st October, 1937, which belonged to a highway, in respect of which the highway authority was not the local sanitary authority,[6] was excluded from the definition of "sewer" contained in section 4 of the 1875 Act,[7] and any such drain did not therefore, vest in the local authority or (now) the water authority as a public sewer under

---

[1] 1936 Act, s. 20 (1) (c).
[2] 1936 Act, s. 20 (1) (b), and proviso to s. 20 (2), in its original form, before the amendment effected by the Water Act, 1973.
[3] Or unless such a declaration had been made by the sanitary authority before 1st April 1974.
[4] 1936 Act, s. 17 (9).
[5] Att.-Gen. v. St. Ives R.D.C. [1961] 1 All E.R. 265.
[6] Apparently a drain "belonging to" a main road which was formerly vested in the county council, and which was transferred to the district council, who were also the local sanitary authority, would not thereby become a public sewer; Williamson v. Durham R.D.C., [1906] 2 K.B. 65. This position is preserved by s. 266 of the Highways Act, 1980.
[7] See Chap. 2, ante, p. 12.

section 20 of the 1936 Act.[1] If the highway of which the drain formed part was vested in or under the control of a highway authority who were also the local sanitary authority, the drain would have been a sewer vested in the local authority (and therefore a public sewer under the 1936 Act) under the 1875 Act in accordance with the normal principles applicable to other drains.[2]

The fact that surface water from a highway was caused to flow into a public sewer would not affect its status,[3] and under section 21 (1) (b) of the 1936 Act, a county council[4] are entitled to use any public sewer vested in the water authority for the conveyance of surface water from roads repairable by them.[5] Similarly any highway drain or sewer[6] may be used by the water authority or by the local authority for the purpose of conveying surface water from premises or streets.[7] Further, the fact that a certain amount of water off a highway flowed into a land drain, would not affect the status of that drain or make it part of the highway.[8] The unauthorised connection of a house drain to a highway drain which is not a public sewer, does not affect the status of the highway drain or cause it to become a public sewer,[9] and a private individual has no right to cause his drains or sewers to be connected therewith, and he would be liable in respect of any nuisance arising as a consequence of any such connection.[10]

---

[1] See Chap. 2, ante, p. 12; and Irving v. Carlisle R.D.C. (1907), 71 J.P. 212.
[2] Chap. 2, ante, p. 11, et seq.
[3] Wilkinson v. Llandaff and Dinas Powis R.D.C., [1903] 2 Ch. 695.
[4] A county council must notify the district council and the water authority: Highways Act, 1980, s. 102 (5) and (6). The Secretary of State has the same powers in respect of a trunk road.
[5] Subject to such terms as may be agreed between the authorities. In default of agreement, the matter may be referred to the Secretary of State, whose decision in the matter is to be final (s. 21(3)).
[6] Vested in the County Council (not the Secretary of State).
[7] P.H.A., 1936, s. 21 (1) (a), as applied by s. 14 (3) of the Water Act 1973; and see footnote [4] above.
[8] Att.-Gen. v. St. Ives R.D.C. [1961] 1 All E.R. 265.
[9] Rickarby v. New Forest R.D.C. (1910), 26 T.L.R. 586.
[10] See, e.g. Wincanton R.D.C. v. Parsons, [1905] 2 K.B. 34.

A "walkway" through a building created by agreement under s. 35 of the Highways Act 1980 or its
predecessor in the Act of 1971, has some of the char-
acteristics of a highway. The agreement made between
the local authority and the owner(s) of the building
should make provision for the drainage of the building
(see section 35 (3) (a), and it is suggested that it should
be made clear that any such drains should remain in
private ownership.

2.   MEANING OF "HIGHWAY DRAIN".

The term "highway drain" is not a term of art, and
yet, for the purpose of deciding questions of liability
for the cleansing thereof, or in respect of accidents
occasioned by such drains, it is important to decide
what forms part of a highway drain and what does not.
As between the highway authority and the water authority, a drain in a highway will be the responsibility
of the former only if it is not a public sewer as above
explained, and if it forms part of the road or highway,
or is vested in the highway authority as such.

Whether or not a particular drain forms part of the
highway, and whether such objects as gullies, gratings
and manhole covers in the highway are part of a drain
belonging to the highway, are questions of fact.[1] Generally speaking, a manhole cover of a public sewer laid

---

[1] See, e.g., Papworth v. Battersea Corporation (No. 2), [1961] 1 K.B. 583.
The question may also arise in connection with private streets not maintainable at the public expense. If the gully forms part of the street, its
cleansing will not be the responsibility of the water authority, but if the
gully is to be regarded as part of the sewer to which it drains, and that
sewer is a public one, the water authority will be responsible for the
cleansing of the gully. "Manholes, ventilating shafts, pumps or other accessories belonging to" the sewer are to be treated as being part thereof for
the purposes of Part II of the 1936 Act, but it is not clear that this expression
includes gullies (see s. 90 (4) of the Act). Again, alterations to the sewerage
system of a private street may be included in private street works expenses
chargeable to the frontagers, but the cost of construction of new gullies
leading to an existing sewer necessitated by the widening of the street, was
held not to be so recoverable from the frontagers, in East Barnet U.D.C.
v. Stacey, [1939] 2 K.B. 861.

under the highway will be treated as part of the sewer and not part of the highway,[1] unless the drain or sewer itself is a highway drain originally constructed solely for the purpose of draining the highway. Gullies and gratings leading to a public sewer, will form part of that sewer,[2] unless they were provided solely for the purpose of draining the highway, in which event they will normally be treated as forming part of the highway.[3]

In a case decided by the Court of Appeal in New Zealand,[4] based on English decisions, it was said that a sewer authority "is not liable in nuisance for the dangerous state of sewers or drains in a highway unless (1) it constructed them, or (2) it is the owner of them, or (3) it has the control or management of them."

3. CLEANSING OF HIGHWAY DRAINS.

Under section 102 of the Highways Act, 1980, the highway authority for a highway may, for the purpose of draining it or of otherwise preventing surface water from flowing on to it, "scour, cleanse, and keep open all drains situated in the highway or in land [adjoining[5] or lying near to the highway]", and they may construct or lay such drains as they consider necessary and divert surface water into or through any existing drain. Any

---

[1] See s. 90 (4) of the 1936 Act (cited in the preceding note), and *Winslow v. Bushey U.D.C.* (1908), 72 J.P. 259, where the local sanitary authority were held liable in respect of an accident which occurred in the highway and was caused by a defective manhole cover forming part of their sewer; but in *Thompson v. Brighton Corporation*, [1894] 1 Q.B. 332, the highway authority were held not liable (in accordance with the principle of non-feasance) nor were the sewer authority, where the cause of the accident was the defective state of the highway surrounding the manhole; and *see* Chap. 3, *ante*, p. 38. Under s. 58 of the Highways Act, 1980, the highway authority can no longer plead non-feasance as a defence, but the special defences in s. 58 (2) of that Act will be relevant.

[2] *White v. Hindley Local Board* (1875), L.R. 10 Q.B. 219.

[3] *Papworth v. Battersea Corporation, supra.* This distinction is, however, by no means clearly drawn in the cases, and the question is essentially one of fact.

[4] *See Patone Borough v. Daubney* [1954] N.Z.L.R. 305, *per* Cooke, J. at page 325.

[5] This includes abutting on: Highways Act, 1980, s. 331 (1).

such water may be discharged into or through the drain and into any inland waters, whether natural or artificial, or any tidal waters. If any owner or occupier of land suffers damage, the authority must pay compensation (to be assessed by arbitration, or, in case of dispute, by the county court).[1]

This useful section confers a power, not a duty, and the highway authority accordingly could not be compelled, by *mandamus* or otherwise, to keep their drains clean, nor were they formerly liable for any nuisance or damage caused by their failure so to do, for such would amount to acts of non-feasance only, for which a highway authority were not liable.[2] The defence of non-feasance is now no longer available to highway authorities,[3] and they are now under an express duty to maintain any highway maintainable at the public expense which is vested in them,[4] and this duty must include, it is submitted, the maintenance of any drains which are part of the highway. An action the damages would therefore lie, it seems at the suit of a person injured by a failure to maintain a highway drain, unless the authority could use one of the defences in s. 58 (2) of the 1980 Act.[5]

The power given by the section also in no way overrides or displaces the common law duty of the owner or occupier of land adjoining the highway so to cleanse and scour any ditches on his land as not to permit them

---

[1] Act of 1980, s. 310.
[2] *See Irving v. Carlisle R.D.C.* (1907), 71 J.P. 212, where the highway authority failed to clean out a ditch and as a result an adjoining occupier sustained damage; and *Masters v. Hampshire C.C.* (1915), 84 L.J.K.B. 2194, where road gullies not connected to any sewer were allowed to become overgrown with grass. In both of these cases, the defendant highway authority were held not liable, the burden of the complaint being in each case based on non-feasance.
[3] Highways Act, 1980, ss. 41 and 58.
[4] *Ibid.*
[5] Following *Griffiths v. Liverpool Corporation* [1967] 1 Q.B. 374, it seems that the authority should institute a proper system of inspection of all highways vested in them, including drains forming part of such highways.

to cause a nuisance on the highway.[1] It is, moreover an offence to alter, obstruct or interfere with any highway drain without the consent of the highway authority.[2]

In cleansing their highway drains, or in causing the surface water to flow off the highway, the highway authority may not cause a nuisance,[3] for here they would be doing positive acts of misfeasance[4]; further, they may not cause or permit any polluted water to flow into a natural stream or watercourse contrary to the Control of Pollution Act 1974.[5]

The expression "drains" used in this section is widely construed by the courts, and a pipe need not be connected to any defined channel for it to be within the section,[6] but a "dumb well" (or "swallow hole", as such a feature is termed in some parts of the country), into which waste water is allowed to flow and there to penetrate into the surrounding soil,[7] or a disused gravel pit or stagnant pond,[8] is not a drain within the section.[9]

---

[1] *Attorney-General v. Waring* (1899), 63 J.P. 789.

[2] Highways Act, 1980, s. 102 (4).

[3] *Pemberton v. Bright* [1960] 1 All E.R. 792, and contrast *Burton v. West Suffolk C. C.* [1960] 2 All E.R. 26. *See also* s. 30 of the 1936 Act, which does not, however, strictly apply in the present context.

[4] *Pearce v. Croydon R.D.C.* (1910). 74 J.P. 429; it will be an actionable nuisance if the surface water off the highway is caused to flow over private land otherwise than in accordance with the existing rights. *See also Thomas v. Gower R.D.C.* (1922), 38 T.L.R. 598.

[5] Water fouled by tar from the surface of the highway was held to be polluted water within this meaning: *Dell v. Chesham U.D.C.*, [1921] 3 K.B. 427. Pure water, or surface water carrying sand or silt, etc., may be discharged into a natural stream: *Durrant v. Branksome U.D.C.*, [1897] 2 Ch. 291. *See also post*, Chap. 8, p. 112.

[6] *Attorney-General v. Copeland*, [1902] 1 K.B. 690.

[7] *Croft v. Rickmansworth Highway Board* (1888), 39 Ch. D. 272.

[8] *Croysdale v. Sunbury-on-Thames U.D.C.*, (1898) 2 Ch. 515.

[9] Therefore the highway authority are not entitled to use such features for the reception of drainage off the highway, except by agreement with the landowners and occupiers concerned. "Unless the pond can be treated as part of the drainage system under the control of the [highway authority], these sections do not empower [the authority] to discharge the surface water into the plaintiff's pond": *per* Stirling, J., in *Croysdale's Case* (note [5] above).

4.   THE SEWERING OF PRIVATE STREETS.

Under Part XI of the Highways Act, 1980,[1] the county council may execute a variety of works in any street which is not a highway maintainable at the public expense, and the cost thereof, provided the procedure of the code is correctly followed, may be charged to the frontagers to the street.[2] It is customary for a number of these works to be done at one and the same time, but this is not an essential feature of the procedure, and any one or more of the works mentioned in the section may be done at one time.[3] One of these works is the "sewering" of the street, where the same is not already sewered to the satisfaction of the authority. There is now no indication as to how "sewer" is to be defined for the purposes of the private street works code contained in the Highways Act, 1980, as the expression is not defined in that Act; formerly the definitions of section 4 of the 1875 Act applied to private street works generally. In practice "sewering" is never regarded as being confined to the provision of a proper system of road drainage for the highway,[4] but includes the provision of a sewer for the drainage from the premises fronting on the street[5] and the expression

---

[1] The code of 1892 was formerly an adoptive Act, which could originally be applied only in urban areas (boroughs and urban districts), but which now applies in all counties, the powers being vested in the county councils: *see* Highways Act, 1980, Part XI, replacing earlier legislation.

[2] "street" is defined in s. 331 (1) of the 1980 Act, and *see also* definition of "private street" in s. 205 (2), *ibid.*

[3] This is clear from the wording of the sections.

[4] A conduit provided for carrying off surface water from roads was held to be a sewer within s. 4 of the 1875 Act, in *Durrant v. Branksome U.D.C.*, [1897] 2 Ch. 291. It might even be arguable that, in view of the absence of any definition "sewer", the provision of road drainage is not included in the term "sewering"; the term "channelling" would, however, appear to be adequate for this purpose. The provision of separate sewers for the reception of sewage and of surface water respectively, is provided for in s. 208 of the 1980 Act.

[5] The authority may, by s. 209 (2) of the 1980 Act, decide to apportion the expenses according to the "degree of benefit" principle, and include premises which do not strictly front on the street, but to which access is obtained from the street.

may include both foul water and surface water conduits.[1] Any sewer constructed under either of these provisions on completion becomes a public sewer, unless it has been constructed by a county council as highway authority.[2].

Once a sewer had been laid in a private street, the construction whereof had been approved by the county council, that council could not subsequently operate these provisions so as to require the provision of a new sewer at the expense of the frontagers,[3] but it must be proved, if these provisions are to be invoked, that the street has at no time been sewered to the satisfaction of the authority.[4]

It is perhaps somewhat anomalous that it is the county council as highway authority who should be able to decide whether or not a street has been sewered to their satisfaction, as the effect of a positive decision to that effect is to vest the sewer not in themselves, but in the water authority. And if arrangements have been made under s. 15 of the Water Act 1973, administration may be undertaken on behalf of the water authority not by the county council, but by the district council. Close co-operatioon between the three authorities will clearly be desirable.

---

[1] In *Bognor Regis U.D.C. v. Boldero* [1962] 2 All E.R. 673, it was held that the magistrates were entitled to determine that the local authority were not acting reasonably where it was proposed to construct two sewers at different times, instead of laying both sewers at the same operation.

[2] 1936 Act, s. 20 (1) (*b*); *see* Chap. 2, *ante*, p. 10.

[3] *Fulham District Board of Works v. Goodwin* (1876), 1 Ex. D. 400; *Bonella v. Twickenham Local Board* (1887), 18 Q.B.D. 577.

[4] It is a question of fact whether or not the authority had in fact been so satisfied, but such will be implied by the court if a reasonable time after the sewer had become vested in the authority they took no action to secure its alteration or re-construction: *Bonella v. Twickenham Local Board (supra)*, and *Wilmslow U.D.C. v. Sidebottom* (1906), 70 J.P. 537. These cases were followed in *Poole Corporation v. Blake*, [1955] 3 W.L.R. 757, when the Court held that s. 9 of the 1892 Act, empowering the local authority to do incidental works as well as those covered by s. 6, *ibid.*, did not have the effect of overruling *Bonella's Case*. In their resolution to sewer the street, the local authority should include a statement to the effect that they were not "satisfied"; *Ware U.D.C. v. Gaunt* [1960] 2 All E.R. 778.

CHAPTER 7

SEWAGE DISPOSAL AND SEWAGE DISPOSAL WORKS

1. INTRODUCTORY.

By virtue of section 14 of the 1973 Act, the water authority are under a duty, not only to drain their area,[1] but also to make "such provision, whether inside or outside their area, by means of sewage disposal works or otherwise, as may be necessary for effectually dealing with the contents of their sewers". The remedies by which this duty may be enforced have been discussed earlier in this book,[2] and it must also be remembered that the functions given by this section may not be exercised by the authority in such a manner as would cause a nuisance.[3] The only practicable methods of dealing with the contents of public sewers are by providing a proper outfall to a river or the sea (provided a nuisance is not thereby cuased, and provided there is no offence against the Control of Pollution Act 1974[4]), or by the provision of disposal works of one type or another.

---

[1] *Cf.* Chap. 3, *ante*, p. 32.
[2] *Ante*, p. 33.
[3] 1936 Act, s. 31. For examples of a nuisance arising out of a sewage farm, *see Bainbridge v. Chertsey U.D.C.* (1914), 84 L.J. Ch. 626, and *Cornford v. Havant and Waterloo U.D.C.* (1933), 31 L.G.R. 142.
[4] There is no common law right to cause the contents of sewers to flow into the sea, if a nuisance is thereby caused: *Foster v. Warblington U.D.C.*, [1906] 1 K.B. 648, and *Hobart v. Southend-on-Sea Corporation* (1906), 75 L.J.K.B. 305. As to the prevention of river pollution, *see post*, Chap. 8, p. 109, *et seq.*, and in particular, *George Legge & Son v. Wenlock Corporation*, [1938] A.C. 204.

2. TRUNK SEWERS.

The provision of a trunk or main sewer is in general governed by the same law as that regulating the provision of all types of public sewers,[1] but in rural localities, the authority may be able to obtain financial assistance not otherwise open to them, under the Rural Water Supplies and Sewerage Acts, 1944 to 1965, as amended by the Water Act 1973, Schedule 8.

Under the 1944 Act,[2] a water authority may obtain a contribution from the Secretary of State (out of moneys provided by Parliament) towards the expenses incurred by them (after the 27th July, 1944[3]), in (*inter alia*) "making adequate provision for the sewerage, or the disposal of the sewage of a rural locality".

The Secretary of State may undertake to make a contribution under this section only on such conditions as the Treasury may determine, and in addition, he must be satisfied that the need for executing the works, etc., proposed, is due to something done or proposed to be done to supply, or to increase the supply of, water in pipes in that locality. After the Secretary of State has agreed to make a contribution under this provision, he may subsequently withhold or reduce the amount of the contribution, if it seems to him that the works have been executed in an unsatisfactory manner, or that the works have not proved substantially as effective as had been estimated, the difference in effectiveness being due to default, for which the water authority were responsible in the formulation of the

---

[1] A main sewer is thus as much a public sewer as is any other sewer constructed by the water authority or its predecessor(s), and private individuals have rights, subject to the authority's powers under s. 34 (3) of the 1936 Act to refuse a communication to be made (*see post*, Chap. 9, p. 121), to cause their house drains to be connected therewith.

[2] *See* s. 1 (1) thereof.

[3] The date of passing the Act.

proposals,[1] or that there has been "any default in the carrying out of the transaction".[2]

There is no longer any duty on the county council to make any contribution towards these expenses as there was under the pre-1974 law.[3]

3. SEWAGE DISPOSAL WORKS.

The power to construct sewage disposal works,[4] is given to a water authority by section 15 (1) (ii) of the 1936 Act, but such works may be constructed only on land acquired or lawfully appropriate for the purpose.[5] If the authority propose to construct any works (which are not included in the extended definition of "sewer", contained in section 90 (4) of the 1936 Act[6]) of sewage disposal,[7] the water authority must therefore either use land already in their ownership, or acquire new land; the special procedure applicable to the laying of a public sewer,[8] whereby no land need be acquired, does not apply to the provision of sewage disposal works. The distinction between "sewers" and "sewage disposal works" was a source of some difficulty in cases decided under the 1875 Act, but the definitions in section 90

---

[1] The authority should therefore carefully consider whether a consultant should be engated to assist in the preparation of any major scheme contemplated under the Acts.

[2] Act of 1944, s. 1 (4).

[3] Section 2 of the 1944 Act has been repealed by the Water Act, 1973, Schedule 8.

[4] The power may not be exercised in such a manner as to cause a nuisance: 1936 Act, s. 31, and *ante*, p. 42. When constructed the works may be equipped with all necessary plant, etc.: *see* 1936 Act, s. 271.

[5] *Sutton v. Norwich Corporation* (1858), 27 L.J. Ch. 739, and *King's College, Cambridge v. Uxbridge R.D.C.*, [1901] 2 Ch. 768.

[6] "Any reference in this Part of this Act to a drain or to a sewer shall be construed as including a reference to any manholes, ventilating shafts, pumps or other accessories belonging to that drain or sewer."

[7] "Sewage disposal works" includes, for the purposes of Part II of the Act, "a reference to the machinery and equipment of those works and any necessary pumping stations and outfall pipes": s. 90 (4) of the 1936 Act.

[8] Chap. 3, *ante*, p. 35 *et seq.*

(4) of the 1936 Act[1] have very largely resolved those difficulties in the present context.[2]

Acquisition of Land.

Acquisition of land for the purpose of construction of sewage disposal works thereon may be by agreement, or by means of a compulsory purchase order made in accordance with the Acquisition of Land (Authorisation Procedure) Act, 1946, the authority for such voluntary or compulsory acquisition being s. 65 of the Water Resources Act, 1963, as applied by s. 9 of the Water Act, 1973.[3] Alternatively, the water authority may be agreement acquire by purchase, lease or otherwise, any existing sewage disposal works,[4] or the right to use any existing sewer or sewage disposal works.[5]

Express planning permission will have to be obtained in respect of any development for the purposes of sewage disposal works, etc., *above* ground level,[6] and, except in so far as the development consists of the laying of sewers or the construction of pumphouses in a line of sewers, or septic tanks and cesspools serving single dwellinghouses or single buildings in which not more than ten persons will normally reside or work, and works ancillary thereto, notices of the proposed development will have to be published pursuant to section 26 of the Town and Country Planning Act, 1971.[7]

---

[1] *See* notes [6] and [7] on p. 102 *ante*.

[2] But *see* below.

[3] Section 306 of the Public Health Act was repealed by the Local Government Act, 1972.

[4] As defined in s. 90 of the 1936 Act: *see* note [7] on preceding page. The works may be either within or outside the authority's area, Act of 1973, Sched. 8 para. 32.

[5] 1936 Act, s. 15 (1) (iii). Where the authority have contracted with a company for the disposal and treatment of their sewage, the company will be liable in nuisance if they do not properly carry out their contract: *Nuneaton Local Board v. General Sewage Co.* (1875), L.R. 20 Eq. 127.

[6] Town and Country Planning General Development Order 1977, First Schedule, Class XVII.

[7] Town and Country Planning General Development Order, 1977, Art. 8 (1) (c).

General Provisions.

Sewage disposal works, like public sewers,[1] may be constructed outside the water authority's area, and the authority may also adopt privately owned sewage disposal works the construction of which had not been completed prior to 1st October, 1937.[2] Section 18 of the 1936 Act, relating to agreements for the adoption of privately owned sewers,[3] applies also to sewage disposal works; similarly, the Public Health Act, 1875 (Support of Sewers) Amendment Act, 1883,[4] applies to sewage disposal works, such works being included in the definition of "sanitary work" contained in that Act.[5]

Ownership.

The following classes of sewage disposal works will be vested in the water authority:

(*a*) Those works which vested in the local authority under the 1875 Act. The term "sewer" as defined in the 1875 Act, did not include an engine house or pumping station,[6] but buildings and works of that nature would none the less have vested in the local sanitary authority under section 13 of the 1875 Act, which operated to vest in the authority all sewers "together with all buildings, works, materials and things belonging thereto".[7]

(*b*) All sewage disposal works[8] constructed by the water authority or their predecessor local authority, or acquired by them.

---

[1] *Ante*, Chap. 2, p. 11; Chap. 3, p. 35.
[2] *See* Chap. 4, *ante*, p. 57.
[3] *Ante*, p. 62.
[4] *Ante*, p. 85.
[5] *See* definition in s. 3 of that Act.
[6] *King's College, Cambridge v. Uxbridge R.D.C.*, [1901] 2 Ch. 768.
[7] A septic tank, filter and outfall privately constructed were held to fall within this expanded definition and to vest in the authority, together with the sewer leading thereto, in *Clark v. Epsom R.D.C.*, [1929] 1 Ch. 287.
[8] *See* expanded definition in s. 90 (4) of the 1936 Act.

(c) All sewage disposal works[7] in respect of which a vesting declaration has been made by the water authority or their predecessor local authority under section 17 of the 1936 Act.[1]

Questions of ownership will arise where the water authority want to use the disposal works as an outfall for a new sewer,[2] or where there is a question as to responsibility for maintenance.[3]

Maintenance.

Having constructed, acquired or otherwise provided, sewage disposal works, it is the duty of the water authority to maintain them in such a manner as not to cause a nuisance,[4] but there is no express statutory duty relating to the cleansing, etc., of sewage disposal works, similar to that imposed by section 23 of the 1936 Act, relating to public sewers.[5]

4. AGREEMENTS WITH OTHER AUTHORITIES.

Besides providing sewage disposal works themselves, or causing the contents of their sewers to flow into the sea or some other natural outfall,[6] a water authority may agree with a neighbouring authority for the disposal of their sewage through the sewerage system of that other authority. The need for such an agreement

---

[1] For these headings, *see* s. 20 of the 1936 Act (as amended).

[2] *Solihull R.D.C. v. Ford* (1932), 30 L.G.R. 385.

[3] *Willoughby v. Chapman*, unreported, but *see* article at (1955), 119 J.P.N. 442.

[4] *See ante*, p. 64, and s. 14 of the 1973 Act and s. 31 of the 1936 Act.

[5] *Ante*, p. 64. It may, therefore, be important to decide whether a particular sewage disposal plant formed part of the sewer under the 1875 Act, and so may be included in a length of sewer to which s. 24 of the 1936 Act applies, or whether it is merely works "belonging to" a sewer and is therefore vested in the authority under s. 13 of the 1875 Act and s. 20 of the 1936 Act, but cannot be regarded as part of the length of sewer within s. 24. A mere catchpit may be part of the sewer (*Pakenham v. Ticehurst R.D.C.* (1903), 67 J.P. 448), but private sewage disposal works will probably be only works "belonging to" the sewer (*Solihull R.D.C. v. Ford* (1932), 30 L.G.R. 385).

[6] *Ante*, p. 100.

is now unlikely, in view of the very extensive areas administered by the water authorities, and there are now no statutory provisions regulating the matter, section 28 of the 1936 Act having been repealed by the 1973 Act.

Apart from statute, the "sending" authority is in the same position as the owner of a dominant tenement in respect of an easement, and can, therefore, only use the sewers of the "receiving" authority by agreement or in pursuance of a prescriptive right so to do.[1]

5.   CONSERVANCY SERVICES.

In addition to the disposal of sewage through a sewerage system, the local authority[2] have duties under the Control of Pollution Act 1974 (replacing the 1936 Act) to arrange for the emptying of all privies[3] serving private dwellings in their area.

In addition, the authority must on request arrange for the emptying of a cesspool[4] in their area which serves only private dwellings. The authority may make no charge for the emptying of such privies, but if they consider appropriate, they may make a reasonable charge for the emptying of cesspools, or any other privy they may agree to empty.[5]

Although the emptying of cesspools, and of privies (other than those serving private dwellings), is a matter

---

[1] *Attorney-General v. Acton Local Board* (1882), 22 Ch. D. 221.
[2] The duties and powers are conferred on the "collection authority"; *i.e.*, district and London borough councils and the Common Council of the City of London.
[3] A "privy" is defined to mean a latrine which has a moveable receptacle for faecal matter.
[4] "Cesspool" includes for this purpose a settlement tank or other tank for the reception or disposal of foul matter from buildings.
[5] Control of Pollution Act, 1974, s. 12 (4). The service may be performed by the local authority themselves, or by their contractor. Where a contractor caused a nuisance through the manner in which he executed his contract to empty cesspools, the employing local authority were held liable: *Robinson v. Beaconsfield U.D.C.*, [1911] 2 Ch. 188.

for arrangement as to the financial terms between the local authority and the occupier requesting the service, it seems that the amount of the charge must not only be reasonable *per se*, but also it must be comparable with charges made for similar services to similar premises.[1]

6. FINANCIAL PROVISIONS.

The financing of the various services provided by local and water authorities that are the subject matter of this book is complicated, and it is here intended to deal with them only in summary fashion.

First, **local** authorities. They draw about half their income from rates, supplemented by exchequer contributions, at present regulated by the Local Government Act 1974. Capital expenditure of any magnitude is financed by way of loans, in respect of which the prior sanction of the Secretary of State is required under section 172 and Schedule 13 of the Local Government Act, 1972. Moneys received from "trading", or by way of charges for services (under, for example, section 12 (4) of the Control of Pollution Act, 1974; must be credited to the general rate fund, pursuant to section 148 (4) of the Local Government Act, 1972; so must any expenses recoverable under statute (for example, under s. 39 of the 1936 Act).

As to **water** authorities, their sewerage expenses will be recovered by charges and schemes made under sections 30 and 31 of the Water Act 1973, and the powers of the former river authorities to precept on local authorities under the Water Resources Act 1963, have been abolished by the 1973 Act. Special charges may be recoverable in respect of the discharge of trade effluent into the water authority's public sewers, but

---

[1] If authority be needed for this proposition, *see* the reasoning in *Pegg & Jones Ltd. v. Derby Corporation* [1909] 2 K.B. 311.

not on a consent granted for the discharge of effluent to a stream (Control of Pollution Act 1974, s. 34 and *see* s. 43 thereof).

The general charges may be collected from the occupiers of premises by the rating authority with the general rates, as agent for the water authority, but it is more common for water authorities to collect the charges (for sewerage, water supply and pollution prevention services) themselves by separate demands. Charges may be made only in respect of services provided, and therefore the occupier of premises not connected to the public sewerage system cannot be charged in respect of sewerage services (although he may be charged for other services provided by the water authority): *Daymond v. South West Water Authority* [1976] 1 All E.R. 39, H.L., and Water Charges Act 1976, section 2.

No exchequer grants are payable to water authorities, except under the Rural Water Supplies and Sewerage Acts, 1944 to 1965 (as amended).[1] Land drainage revenue may be raised by land drainage rates and by precepts on local authorities as in the past. After 31st March 1978, charges may be substituted therefor. A water authority has power to raise capital money by way of loan in accordance with, but only in accordance with, paragraph 34 of Schedule 3 to the Water Act 1973; subject to the consent of the Secretary of State.

Under the Water Charges Equalisation Act 1977, a water authority may be required, by directions made by the Secretary of State, to pay an equalisation levy to the National Water Council, who may then be required to make payments to other water authorities.

---

[1] *Ante*, p. 101. In addition, grants may be made from Treasury funds under para. 35 of Schedule 3 to the Water Act 1973.

CHAPTER 8

THE DISCHARGE OF SEWAGE EFFLUENTS

1. INTRODUCTORY.

In this Chapter it is intended to deal with the discharge of effluents (either treated or untreated) from public sewers or sewage disposal works vested in the water authority; discharge of effluents from private premises into public sewers is discussed in other parts of this book, but we shall also deal here with discharges from private premises otherwise than to public sewers. Discharge of sewage effluents can be, in the nature of things, only to a watercourse or to the sea, and these will be dealt with separately. Discharge from public sewers to a watercourse does not now give rise to any very complicated problems, in view of the Control of Pollution Act, 1974.

2. DISCHARGES TO A WATERCOURSE: STATUTORY PROVISIONS.

The Act of 1974 makes it illegal to cause[1] or permit the discharge of sewage effluent into relevant waters,[2] into the sea from land in Great Britain through a pipe, or from a building or plant into or onto any land, lake, loch or pond; unless the discharge is made with the

---

[1] If the water authority was bound to receive matter included in a discharge of sewage effluent which is then discharged by them into relevant waters, etc., the water authority is to be deemed to have caused the discharge: 1974 Act, s. 32 (2).

[2] "Relevant waters" for the purposes of this Act means any "stream" (defined to include any river, watercourse or inland water except tidal waters and ponds, etc), controlled waters (the sea within a three mile territorial limit) and any underground water specified in a report made by the water authority (see Act of 1974, ss. 56 (1) and 31 (1)).

consent of the water authority[1]; and this provision has effect subject to regulations made by the Secretary of State in relation to discharges made by water authorities.[2]

This provision applies to private individuals and limited companies, and also to local authorities. Moreover, by s. 31 of the 1974 Act it is illegal for any person to cause or knowingly permit to enter relevant waters any poisonous, noxious or polluting matter, or to cause or knowingly permit to enter a stream any matter so as to tend either directly or in combination with similar acts (whether his own or another's) to impede the proper flow of the water of the stream in a manner leading or likely to lead to a substantial aggravation of pollution [a term which is not defined in the Act] due to other causes or of its consequences, or to cause, etc., any solid waste to enter a stream, etc. It is a defence to a charge under this section to show that the discharge was made pursuant to a disposal licence granted by the disposal authority (the county council or in Wales the district council) under Part I of the 1974 Act, or pursuant to a consent granted by the water authority under Part II of that Act. There are also other defences available in case of emergency or if it can be shown the discharge was made in accordance with a good agricultural practice which has not been expressly forbidden by notice under s. 46 of the 1974 Act.

Consents to discharges under either s. 31 or s. 32 will normally be given only subject to conditions, and therefore any new or altered discharge will need either a new consent or a variation of the conditions in an existing consent.

Any such consent of the water authority may not be

---

[1] Act of 1974, s. 32.
[2] *Ibid.*, s. 55.

unreasonably withheld, and any question as to whether or not such consent has been unreasonably withheld in a particular case is to be determined by reference to the Secretary of State.[1] A consent may impose conditions, and these conditions must be recorded in a register maintained by the water authority.[2]

Section 4 of the Salmon and Freshwater Fisheries Act, 1975, also prohibits the putting into any waters containing fish, or into any tributaries thereof, "any liquid or solid matter to such an extent as to cause the waters to be poisonous or injurious to fish or the spawning grounds, spawn or food of fish".

Further, section 30 of the 1936 Act (as amended by the Water Act, 1973) provides that "Nothing in [Part II] of this Act shall authorise a water authority to construct or use any public or other sewer, or any drain or outfall, for the purpose of conveying foul water [not necessarily sewage matter] into any natural or artificial stream,[3] watercourse, canal, pond or lake, until the water has been so treated as not to affect prejudicially the purity and quality of the water in the stream, watercourse, canal, pond or lake". Section 31 of the same Act (as amended) provides that a water authority must so exercise their functions under the said Part II of the Act (which includes the provisions requiring them to sewer their area) as not to cause a nuisance. The common law regarding the rights of riparian owners to have an unpolluted flow of water, where such have been acquired by grant or by prescription (*see* below), are preserved by section 331 of the 1936 Act, which pro-

---

[1] Control of Pollution Act, 1974, s. 39.

[2] In accordance with regulations made by the Secretary of State; *ibid*, s. 41.

[3] This term is not defined in the 1936 Act, and the definition of the 1974 Act does not apply. Periodic flooding in no particular defined channel was held not to amount to a "natural stream or watercourse" within s. 17 of the 1875 Act (the predecessor, in somewhat different words of the present section), in *Pearce v. Croydon R.D.C.* (1910), 74 J.P. 429, and *see also Maxwell-Willshire v. Bromley R.D.C.* (1918), L.J. Ch. 241.

vides that nothing in that Act shall authorise an authority injuriously to affect any watercourse, etc., or the supply, quality or fall of water therein, without the consent of any person who would, if the Act had not been passed, have been entitled to prevent or to be relieved against any such injurious affection.

These provisions are not directly affected by the Act of 1974, nor do they afford any defence to contraventions against its provisions, but it has been suggested that section 31 gives an implied right (if such a right be needed) to cause harmless effluent to flow from a sewer into a stream or watercourse.[1]

Under section 33 of the Control of Pollution Act 1974, a water authority may make byelaws controlling the use of sanitary appliances in vessels (including hovercraft) on a stream or "restricted waters" (*see* s. 56 (1)).

3.   DISCHARGES TO A WATERCOURSE: COMMON LAW.

Quite apart from statutory provisions, the discharge of sewage effluent or other polluting matter into any stream may amount to a nuisance in respect of which a riparian owner may take proceedings at common law for an injunction and/or for damages. The pollution need not be so bad as to amount to a public nuisance, as any riparian owner is entitled to have a flow of water in any natural stream which is in all respects in its natural state; a similar right may attach to an artificial stream, if the right has been acquired by grant or by prescription. At common law pollution means the addition of something to water which changes its natural qualities, such as the addition of hard water to soft water, the raising of the temperature of the water, or

---

[1] *Durrant v. Branksome* U.D.C., [1896] 2 Ch. 291. decided on the corresponding section in the 1875 Act.

the addition of something which on meeting some other substance already in the water, each in themselves harmless, causes pollution.[1]

Compliance with the provisions of the Control of Pollution Act 1974, will be no defence in common law proceedings. The standards of the common law, as several local authorities learnt to their cost, are higher than those so far imposed by Parliament; seemingly harmless extraneous matter is none the less capable of being treated as pollution at common law. On the other hand an injunction is a discretionary remedy, and it would not be granted by a court where no prejudice whatever can be shown to the plaintiff's interests.[2]

The fact that the water authority have not themselves taken any active steps which have caused the common law nuisance in question will also be no defence; they are expressly prohibited from causing a nuisance in the exercise of their functions by section 31 of the Act of 1936, and non-feasance is no excuse.[3] The fact that the particular watercourse was already polluted from some other source would also be no defence in such proceedings.[4]

It used to be said that at common law a right to pollute a watercourse could be acquired by prescription or by grant as an easement as against a riparian pro-

---

[1] See Coulson & Forbes on Waters and Land Drainage, 6th edn., at p. 198, and Crossley v. Lightowler (1866), L.R. 2 Ch. 476, and other cases there cited. In Young & Co. v. Bankier Distillery Co., [1893] A.C. 691, Lord Macnaghten said (at p. 698), "A riparian owner is entitled to have the water of the stream, on the banks of which his property lies, flow down as it has been accustomed to flow down to his property, subject to the ordinary use of the flowing water by upper proprietors, and to such further use, if any, on their part in connection with their property as may be reasonable in the circumstances. Every riparian proprietor is thus entitled to the water of his stream, in its natural flow, without sensible diminution or increase and without sensible alteration in its character or quality".

[2] Kensit v. G.E. Rlwy. Co. (1884), 27 Ch. D. 122.

[3] Pride of Derby and Derbyshire Angling Assn. v. British Celanese, [1953] 2 W.L.R. 58.

[4] See Wright v. Williams (1836), 1 M. & W. 77.

prietor lower down the watercourse,[3] but where such pollution would constitute an offence against the 1974 Act (and a similar principle applied under the earlier statutes), it seems that such a right would not now be upheld by the courts.

4. STATUTORY NUISANCES.

In addition to the above restrictions, statutory or common law, on pollution of watercourses and streams, certain matters are expressly dealt with by section 259 of the 1936 Act. These provisions are enforceable not by the water authority, but by the local authority. The section provides that the following are statutory nuisances:

"(a) any pond, pool, ditch, gutter or watercourse which is so foul or in such a state as to be prejudicial to health or a nuisance[1];

(b) any part of a watercourse, not being a part ordinarily navigated by vessels, employed in the carriage of goods by water, which is so choked or silted up as to obstruct or impede the proper flow of water and thereby to cause a nuisance, or give rise to conditions prejudicial to health[2];

Provided that in the case of an alleged nuisance under para. (b), nothing in this subsection shall be deemed to impose any liability on any person other than the person by whose act or default the nuisance arises or continues."

In order therefore, for a local authority to operate the "nuisance clauses" (sections 92 to 100 of the 1936

---

[1] *Att.-Gen. v. Leeds Corporation* (1870), 5 Ch. App. 583.
[2] "Prejudicial to health" is defined by s. 343 (1) of the 1936 Act to mean "injurious, or likely to cause injury to health". It is not necessary to prove that a particular state of affairs is *both* a nuisance and injurious to health: *Betts v. Penge U.D.C.*, [1942] 2 All E.R. 61, and see *post*, page 141.

Act; and one local authority may take statutory action against another under these provisions[1]) in respect of para. (*b*), the actual offender must be discovered, either *flagrante delicto*, or by establishing that he has failed to perform a legal duty already imposed on him to clear out the watercourse in question. A riparian owner is not normally under an express (or implied) duty to clear out a natural stream,[2] and in practice it may well be difficult to prove a sufficient act or default to bring a defendant within the proviso to the present section.

Ancillary powers with regard to watercourses, ditches, etc., are given to the local authority by sections 260 to 266 of the 1936 Act, and these are not affected by the 1974 Act, or by the Water Act 1973, although in other respects, prevention of river pollution functions are vested in the water authorities constituted under the Water Act, 1973.

5. DISCHARGE TO THE SEA.

At common law there is no right for a local authority, or any person, to discharge sewage or any polluting matter into the sea, and an injunction may be granted if a nuisance is caused by any such discharge, at the instance of the person injured.[3] On the other hand, if the discharge is effected in such a manner as to obviate any nuisance, no legal proceedings could be taken.

Section 32 of the Control of Pollution Act 1974, as

---

[1] *R. v. Epping Justices ex p. Burlinson*, [1947] 2 All E.R. 537.
[2] *Neath R.D.C. v. Williams*, [1951] 1 K.B. 115, following *Hodgson v. York Corporation* (1873), 37 J.P. 325. Very different considerations apply if the defendant creates an artificial watercourse or does anything to make artificial that which was previously natural: *Sedleigh-Denfield v. O'Callaghan*, [1940] A.C. 880.
[3] *Hobart v. Southend-on-Sea Corporation* (1906), 75 L.J.K.B. 305, and *Foster v. Warblington U.D.C.*, [1906] 1 K.B. 648. A local authority may themselves be in the position of plaintiffs where their property has been injured as the consequence of pollution of the sea or tidal waters: *Esso Petroleum Co. Ltd. v. Southport Corporation*, [1956] 2 W.L.R. 81.

above mentioned, makes it an offence, without the consent of the water authority, to discharge sewage effluent into controlled waters or into the sea outside the three mile limit by means of a pipe from land in Great Britain.

Every accretion from the sea, whether natural or artificial, any part of the sea-shore to the low-water mark, forms part of the district of the local authority whose area it adjoins,[1] but section 340 of the Public Health Act, 1936, provides that a local authority or water authority may not execute any works below high water mark without the approval of the Secretary of State for Trade and Industry.

It should also be noted that a local fisheries committee for a sea fisheries district may make byelaws prohibiting or regulating the deposit or discharge of any solid or liquid substance detrimental to sea fish or sea fishing under section 5 (1) (c) of the Sea Fisheries Regulation Act, 1966. Section 4 of the Salmon and Freshwater Fisheries Act, 1975,[2] may also apply to particular tidal waters.[3] The discharge of oil[4] or any mixture containing oil into U.K. territorial waters or navigable internal waters, or from a "place" on land (which would presumably include a sewer), constitutes an offence against section 2 of the Prevention of Oil Pollution Act 1971.

---

[1] Local Government Act, 1972, s. 72.
[2] *See* p. 111, *supra*.
[3] Water Resources Act, 1963, s. 9 (1).
[4] "Oil" is defined, somewhat loosely, in s. 29 (1) of the 1971 Act.

CHAPTER 9

DRAINAGE OF PREMISES

1. INTRODUCTORY.

In this chapter it is proposed to deal mainly with drains, as distinct from sewers, and in particular with the drainage of individual buildings and other premises.

In practice, care has to be exercised to consider whether the particular statutory function in question is exercisable by the water authority or by the local authority. In general,[1] matters related to a public sewer are the concern of the water authority, while matters relating exclusively to drains are the concern of the local authority.

Drains are not vested in the water or local authority (except where they are owners of property served thereby), but it is the concern of the local authority to ensure that proper means of drainage are provided for new buildings, and that the drains of existing buildings do not cause a nuisance, and also that their contents do not injure the public sewers into which the drains—mediately or immediately—discharge. It is also necessary to consider the circumstances in which the owner or occupier of a building may cause his drains or sewers to be connected to the public sewer vested in the water authority, and the use that may be made of any drains so connected.

---

[1] But see detailed table, post, p. 188.

2. RIGHTS TO CONNECT DRAINS TO PUBLIC SEWERS.

(a) The nature of the rights.

Under section 34 of the 1936 Act as amended by s. 14 (4) of the Act of 1973, the owner[1] or occupier of any premises,[2] or the owner of any private sewer[3] is entitled to have his drains or sewer made to communicate with the public sewers of any water authority, provided he has the right (by virtue of ownership or easements) to cause his drain or sewer to pass through the intervening land, and he may thereby discharge foul and surface water from those premises or that private sewer; the right does not, however, apply to a sewer vested in the authority which has not become a public sewer. Subject to the restrictions mentioned below, and to the prescribed procedure being observed, this right is absolute (the owner or occupier exercising the right must act, however, at his expense), and the person exercising such right will not be responsible if the public sewer is not properly maintained or has an inadequate outfall, or connects with a stream in such a manner as to offend against the Control of Pollution Act, 1974.[4] Under the 1875 Act, it was held that once a communication had been lawfully made under the statutory power which

---

[1] Defined in s. 343 (1) of the Act.

[2] The definition of this term in s. 343 (1) is wide enough to include open land, and such premises as caravan sites or factories. However, it is clear that the right of s. 34 extends only to "drains and sewers", and those are defined (again in s. 343 (1)) in relation to buildings. If there is a conduit from a caravan site there will normally be a building although possibly a mere effluent pipe for sullage is not a "drain". It is also clear that s. 34 cannot be used as a claim to connect a land drain to a public sewer.

[3] This also is defined in s. 343 (1), as any sewer which is not a public sewer.

[4] See ante, Chap. 8, p. 109. This does not mean, however, that a particular effluent which would offend against the Act, when it reached the stream may be discharged into the sewer (see proviso (a) (ii) to the present section, below), but that if the effluent from the sewer already pollutes that stream, a particular owner or occupier of premises discharging into the sewer will not be held responsible. On the general principle, see Ainley & Sons Ltd. v. Kirkheaton L.B. (1891), 60 L.J. Ch. 734, and Brown v. Dunstable Corporation, [1899] 2 Ch. 378.

was the predecessor of the present section,[1] any type of effluent (not injurious to health) could be discharged into the public sewer.[2] On the other hand in two cases[3] in both of which no notice had been given to the local authority pursuant to section 21 of the 1875 Act,[4] a right claimed to connect a foul water drain with a highway (public) sewer, or to change the nature of the effluent to such a sewer from slops to faecal matter, was denied by the court. It is not clear that the decisions would have been the same if the statutory procedure had been followed, but it may be possible to argue that a sewer designed (*e.g.*) for slop water only cannot be used for other purposes.

Under the 1936 Act, there are a number of specific restrictions as to what may be discharged to a public sewer, and some such sewers may be reserved for foul, or for surface water[5] respectively. Subject to the restrictions, it seems that any effluent coming within this expression may be discharged into the public sewer without the consent of the water authority.

Section 34 provides that this right shall not entitle any person:

> "(*a*) to discharge directly or indirectly into any public sewer—
>
> > (i) any liquid from a factory,[6] other than domestic sewage or surface water or

---

[1] Act of 1875, s. 21.

[2] *See* the judgment of Charles, J., in *Peebles v. Oswaldtwistle U.D.C.*, [1897] 1 Q.B. 384, at p. 392.

[3] *Kinson Pottery Co. v. Poole Corporation*, [1899] 2 Q.B. 41, and *Graham v. Wroughton*, [1901] 2 Ch. 451.

[4] The predecessor to s. 34 (3) of the 1936 Act.

[5] "Surface water" is defined by s. 90 (1) of the 1936 Act for the present purpose as including "water from roofs".

[6] This term is to be understood as defined by s. 175 of the Factories Act, 1961; *see* s. 343 (1) of the 1936 Act, and s. 184 (1) of the Factories Act, 1961.

storm water, or any liquid from a man-
ufacturing process[1]; *or*

(ii) any liquid or other matter the discharge
of which into public sewers is prohibited
by or under any enactment (including
any enactment in this Act[2]); *or*

(*b*) where separate public sewers are provided
for foul water and for surface water,[3] to discharge directly or indirectly—

(i) foul water into a sewer provided for surface water; or

(ii) except with the approval of the [water]
authority, surface water into a sewer
provided for foul water; or

(*c*) to have his drains or sewer made to communicate directly with a storm-water overflow sewer.[4]"

It should also be noted that the right relates only to
communications to be made from a drain or sewer as
defined in the 1936 Act, which would exclude land or
agricultural drains, and any person making a communication with a public sewer must comply with the
provisions of the section (*see* section 34 (5)).

(b) How the rights may be exercised.
In order that a person may exercise the rights given
by this section, he must give the water authority prior

---

[1] But *see* the Public Health (Drainage of Trade Premises) Act, 1937,
below, p. 145, and in particular, the definition therein of "trade effluent".

[2] The reference here is to s. 27 of the 1936 Act (set out in Chap. 5, *ante*,
p. 88), or possibly to the Public Health (Drainage of Trade Premises) Act,
1937; *see* s. 14 (2) thereof. "Enactment" would also include the Control of
Pollution Act 1974 (Chap. 8, *ante*, p. 109), and any relevant local Acts.

[3] Under s. 22 of the 1936 Act, the authority may prohibit the use of any
public sewer either entirely, or for the purpose of foul water drainage, or
for the purpose of surface water drainage (and *see* Chap. 5, *ante*, p. 88).

[4] 1936 Act, s. 34, proviso. This expression is not defined in the Act.

written notice[1] of the proposals, and at any time within 21 days of the receipt of such notice, the authority may by notice[2] refuse to permit the communication to be made, "if it appears to them that the mode of construction or condition of the drain or sewer is such that the making of the communication would be prejudicial to their sewerage system,[3] and for the purpose of examining the mode of construction and condition of the drain or sewer they may, if necessary, require it to be laid open for inspection[4]".

Any person wishing to exercise the rights given by the section may appeal to the local magistrates' court[5] against any refusal of the authority to permit the communication to be made,[6] and the authority will then have to justify their contention that the communication would prejudice their system, or (as the case may be), that the person concerned is not entitled to use the section as one or other of the above restrictions applies. Similarly, an appeal lies to the magistrates[2] if any question arises as to the reasonableness of the requirements

---

[1] The notice must be in writing and duly signed and served in accordance with ss. 283 to 285; these sections are applied to water authorities by s. 14 (1) of the 1973 Act. The form need not follow any particular wording, but Shaw's Form PH 58 is appropriate.

[2] This also must be in writing and duly signed and served (*see* preceding note); Shaw's Form PN 12 is appropriate.

[3] There is no explanation of this expression afforded by the Act. Clearly the subsection could be invoked to prevent (for example) a 12-inch private sewer being connected to a 4-inch public sewer, but it is doubtful, especially in view of *Smeaton v. Ilford Corporation*, [1954] 1 All E.R. 923, *ante*, p. 43, whether the power could be used where it is alleged that the effluent to be discharged into the sewer would surcharge the sewer or otherwise cause a nuisance.

[4] 1936 Act, s. 34 (3). The requirements of the authority should, it is submitted (although this is not expressly stipulated in the statute), be notified in writing; Shaw's Form PN 13 is appropriate.

[5] An appeal lies by a "party aggrieved" from the decision of the magistrates to the Crown Court: 1936 Act, s. 301.

[6] There is, however, no right of appeal to the magistrates against a refusal to make a communication with a main sewer in Greater London: Water Act 1973, Schedule 8, para. 37. "Main sewer" for this purpose means a public sewer used for reception of sewage from other public sewers: *ibid*

of the authority regarding the opening of the drain or sewer in question.[1]

If the communication is made without such notice having been given to the water authority, the person responsible will be liable to a fine, and the authority will be entitled to close the communication so made and recover their expenses from the person responsible.[2]

(c) The making of the communication.

The physical work of making the communication with the public sewer may be executed by the owner or occupier concerned, unless, within 14 days of the notice of his proposals having been served on the water authority as above mentioned,[3] the authority have given notice[4] to such person to the effect that they themselves intend to make the communication.[5]

Whichever party actually executes the works, the provisions of the Public Utilities Street Works Act, 1950,[6] and Part VI of the Third Schedule to the Water Act, 1945,[7] relating to the breaking-up of streets will apply thereto.[8]

Where the owner or occupier decides to execute the work of communication himself, he must, before commencing the work, "give reasonable notice[9] to any person directed by the authority to superintend the execution of the work and afford him all reasonable

---

[1] 1936 Act, s. 34 (3), proviso.
[2] 1936 Act, s. 34 (5).
[3] Or within 14 days of the determination of any question by the court.
[4] This notice must be in writing and duly signed and served (1936 Act, ss. 283 to 285, applied by s. 14 (2) of the Water Act 1973).
[5] 1936 Act, s. 36 (1).
[6] This Act repeals s. 279 (3) of the 1936 Act, and lays down a procedure to be observed for "code-regulated" street works, etc.
[7] Applied by s. 279 (1) of the 1936 Act, as amended by the 1945 Act.
[8] 1936 Act, s. 34 (2), and s. 36 (4).
[9] This notice must be in writing and duly served: 1936 Act, ss. 283 and 285.

facilities for superintending the execution thereof[1]". If the work is executed by some person other than the authority (or on their behalf) it may be necessary to obtain the consent of the owner of any intervening land, but probably not to take the drain through the subsoil of a private street, whether this is a highway or not.[2]

Where the water authority have given notice to the effect that they intend to execute the work of making the communication, they have "all such rights in respect of the making of the communication as the person desiring it to be made would have[3]", but they are entitled to ask for the cost of the work, as estimated by their surveyor, to be paid to them, or security for payment given to their satisfaction, before they commence to do the work.[4] If any payment so made in advance exceeds the expenses reasonably incurred[5] by the authority in the execution of the work, they must repay the excess, and if and so far as their expenses[6] are not covered by any payment, they may recover the

---

[1] 1936 Act, s. 34 (4).

[2] See the wide definition of "street" in s. 343 (1) of the 1936 Act, and the remarks of Lord Hanworth, M.R., in *Grant v. Derwent* [1929] 1 Ch. 390, at p. 397.

[3] This would include, *e.g.*, the right to enter on private land without payment of compensation, but only where that right is vested in the person in whose place they are acting: see *Wood v. Ealing Tenants Ltd.*, [1907] 2 K.B. 390, decided under the earlier legislation. The powers of s. 15 and s. 287 (1) of the 1936 Act would not apply to such a case. If the private owner has no right to cause his drain to run through land belonging to some other person but lying between the premises to be drained and the public sewer, the communication cannot be made. A similar position obtains if the water authority act by agreement under s. 275 of the Act.

[4] 1936 Act, s. 36 (2). Having given such notice, it seems that they could be compelled by mandamus to do the work.

[5] A reasonable sum by way of establishment expenses may be included: Local Government Act 1974, s. 36, applied by s. 14 (2) of the Water Act 1973.

[6] *I.e.*, their reasonable expenses, plus establishment expenses.

expenses, or the balance thereof, from the person for whom the work was done.[1].

The water authority are not obliged to recover such expenses (or all of them); section 13 of the Local Government (Miscellaneous Provisions) Act, 1953, has legalised the practice whereby some authorities pay for the cost of the "laterals"; *i.e.*, that part of the drain which lies between the public sewer and the boundary of the street.[2] An authority may also use this section to construct at their own expense, such laterals as they may anticipate will be required, at the time when they construct a sewer.

(d) Communications outside the area.

There is now no distinction between communications with sewers inside or outside an authority's area, and section 35 of the P.H.A. 1936 has been repealed by the Water Act 1973.

(e) Offences.

It is expressly made an offence to cause a drain or sewer to communicate with a public sewer without complying with the procedure of section 34 of the 1936 Act, or before the expiration of 21 days after the receipt by the authority of the notice of proposals under section 34 (3).[3] It is also an offence to proceed to make such a communication after a notice has been given to

---

[1] The means of recovery will be as for a civil debt under s. 294 of the 1936 Act, or by simple action in the local county court (unless the amount claimed exceeds £750, in which event the action will have to be brought in the High Court); and *see* Chap. 11, *post*, p. 176.

[2] Even where this is done, the fact that the lateral is constructed at the authority's expense does not, it is submitted, make it a public sewer under s. 20 (1) (*b*) of the 1936 Act, as a lateral is not a "sewer" unless it is designed to serve more than one premises.

[3] If a person fails to serve proper notice as required by the section, he will not be able to plead the section as a defence in nuisance proceedings brought as a consequence of the connection of his drains to the sewer: *Graham v. Wroughton*, [1901] 2 Ch. 451.

the effect that the authority intend to make the communication themselves.[1]

(f) Rights, not Duties.

The power to communicate with a public sewer is a right, and not a duty. The water authority (or the local authority) cannot, therefore, require the owner or occupier of premises to cause his drains to communicate with a public sewer, unless it can be said that "satisfactory provision has not been made for drainage" of the building, and that the only means of so providing would be by making such communication[2]; and in such an event action would have to be taken by the local authority, not the water authority. Thus, where premises are drained to a cesspit, which is in good order and adequate for the purpose, neither authority can, except by offering to pay the cost thereof,[3] require the cesspit to be abolished and main drainage substituted therefor. The local authority would also not be entitled to refuse to cleanse a cesspool or empty a privy, as a means of putting pressure on the owner of the premises to cause them to be communicated with the public sewer.[4]

3. THE DRAINAGE OF NEW BUILDINGS.

The Act of 1936 gives an effective means of control over the type of drainage proposed for a new building, but as this is exercised by the local authority (and *not* the water authority) through the medium of the Building Regulations, 1976, it is first important to appreciate the types of work to which, and the circumstances in which, this control is applicable.

---

[1] 1936 Act, s. 36 (1).

[2] *See* s. 39 of the 1936 Act, *infra*, p. 138.

[3] *See* s. 42 of the 1936 Act (a section administered by the water authority: *post*, p. 134), but apart from that section, the authority have no power under the Act to contribute towards the cost of private sewerage works.

[4] Under s. 14 of the Control of Pollution Act, 1974, *ante*, p. 106.

(a) When the control is effective.

In the first place, the control over the drainage of new buildings herein discussed depends on the terms of the Regulations, which apply only with respect to the design and construction of buildings,[1] and alterations and extensions of buildings, and also to the provision of services, fittings or equipment in or in connection with buildings (P.H.A., 1936, ss. 61 and 62, as re-written by the Health and Safety at Work, etc., Act 1974[2]). Control in practice is most effective where plans are required to be submitted before the work is commenced, but these have to be submitted only where the Building Regulations so provide.[3] Where a building is totally exempt from this control,[4] this section also is inoperative.

(b) Drainage provisions.

Apart from specific breaches of the express requirements of the Regulations, it is also an offence to fail to submit plans (where these are required), before commencing the work, and where the plans provide for the drainage of a building the local authority has power to order the demolition of works executed prior to the submission of plans, even if such work does not in fact contravene the section.[5]

When plans are received by the local authority, they must be considered, and if they contravene the provisions of the Building Regulations, or of the 1936 Act, the authority must reject the plans, and give notice of

---

[1] "Building" is not defined in the Act, but its usual meaning as any construction or erection capable of enclosing an area of ground, would seem to apply in this context, and in particular, it must be "some structure contemplated by and dealt with in the byelaws": *Slaughter v. Sunderland Corporation* (1891), 60 L.J.M.C. 91, and contrast the meaning of the expression for the purposes of s. 25 of the 1936 Act, *ante*, Chap. 5, p. 82.

[2] This Act is not yet fully in force, and it cannot be effective until new Building Regulations have been made thereunder.

[3] 1936 Act, s. 61 (4), as amended.

[4] *See* 1936 Act, s. 71 and Building Regulation A 4 (1).

[5] 1936 Act, s. 65 (2), read with s. 37 (1).

such rejection to the building owner.[1] If such notice of rejection is not served within the prescribed period,[2] the plans cannot subsequently be rejected, but failure to serve notice of rejection does not of itself legalise any contravening work, but merely destroys the right of the authority to require the building owner to remove the contravening work.[3] Similarly, approval of work which contravenes the Building Regulations does not legalise such work, but the authority again lose their powers to order removal.[4]

The authority have no discretion, as has a local planning authority acting under the Town and Country Planning Act, 1971, whether to pass or reject plans[5]; if the Regulations or the Act are contravened, the plans must be rejected; however, if the provisions of the Regulations would be unreasonable in relation to a particular case, they may be dispensed with or relaxed by direction made by the Secretary of State or the local authority.[6] Further, plans of a building or of an extension of a building must be rejected "unless either the plans show that satisfactory provision will be made for the drainage of the building[7] or of the extension, as the case may be, or the local authority are satisfied that in

---

[1] 1936 Act, s. 64. The notice must be in writing, and duly signed and served, in accordance with ss. 283 to 285; Shaw's Form BR 7 is appropriate.

[2] Five weeks, or such extended period (not more than 2 months from the deposit of the plans) as may be agreed: P.H.A., 1936, s. 64 (4), as amended by P.H.A., 1961, s. 10 (2).

[3] 1936 Act, s. 65 (2).

[4] In either case, the authority may still prosecute for an offence against the Regulations. They may also take proceedings for an injunction in the High Court, but in these circumstances the court may order the authority to pay compensation to the building owner: s. 65 (5).

[5] It seems that the Secretary of State will not support a decision under the Town and Country Planning Act, 1971, refusing planning permission for the erection of a single dwelling solely on the ground that satisfactory provision is not proposed to be made for the drainage thereof; this is a matter to be controlled under the public health legislation and not under the Planning Act: see article at (1959), J.P.L. 236.

[6] 1961 Act, s. 6.

[7] "Drainage" for the purposes of the section is defined to include "the conveyance, by means of a sink and any other necessary appliance, of refuse water and the conveyance of rain water from roofs"; s. 37 (1).

the case of the particular building or extension they may properly dispense with any provision for drainage[1]". This provision merits more detailed consideration.

(i) *"Satisfactory provision."* The local authority must be satisfied that satisfactory provision has been made, and, subject to compliance with the section, it seems that the magistrates' court (on appeal to them under the section) is not entitled to substitute its decision for that of the authority, provided there were grounds on which the latter could reasonably have come to their decision. The provision referred to is only for the drainage of the particular building and the authority cannot reject the plans because the sewerage system into which the drains (otherwise satisfactory) are to discharge, is unsatisfactory.[2]

Section 37 (3) of the Act provides that a proposed drain is not to be deemed to be satisfactory for the purposes of this section, unless it is proposed to be made, as the local authority[3] may require, "either to connect with a sewer,[4] or to discharge into a cesspool[5] or into some other place".

The authority may not[6] require a drain to be made to connect to a sewer[7] **unless**:—

---

[1] 1936 Act, s. 37 (1).

[2] *Chesterton R.D.C. v. Ralph Thompson, Ltd.*, [1947] 1 All E.R. 273; "I think, therefore, that quarter sessions were right in coming to the conclusion that the only matter they had to consider was the suitability of the particular drain which connects with the sewer and they were not concerned with what happens to the drainage of the houses once it passes into the sewer or whether the sewer itself is satisfactory": *per* Lord Goddard, C.J.

[3] Or the magistrates' court on appeal to them under the section.

[4] Not necessarily a public sewer.

[5] "Cesspool" is defined for the purposes of Part II of the 1936 Act by s. 90 (1) thereof, as *including* "a settlement tank or other tank for the reception or disposal of foul matter from buildings", but the term is not, it seems, thereby confined to receptacles for foul matter.

[6] Subject to their agreeing to pay the extra cost as mentioned below.

[7] Not necessarily a public sewer.

"(a) that sewer is within one hundred feet[1] of the site of the building or, in the case of an extension, the site either of the extension or of the original building, and is at a level which makes it reasonably practicable to construct a drain to communicate therewith, and, if it is not a public sewer, is a sewer which the person constructing the drain is entitled to use[2]; **and**

(b) the intervening land is land through which that person is entitled to construct a drain."

On the other hand, if the authority require a connection to be made to a sewer which is not within the distance of one hundred feet above-mentioned, the authority must then undertake to "bear so much of the expenses reasonably incurred in constructing, and in maintaining and repairing, the drain as may be attributable to the fact that the distance of the sewer exceeds" that distance.[3] Such a requirement and undertaking are not matters of routine administration, and therefore they must be embodied in a formal resolution of the council if they are to be effective.[4]

(ii) *Combined drains.* The above provision, like its predecessor in the 1875 Act,[5] enables the authority to insist on a separate drain being provided for each build-

---

[1] The measurements must be taken "in a straight line on a horizontal plane": Interpretation Act, 1978, s. 8. The hundred feet is to be measured, not from the curtilege, but the site of the building drained, *Meyrick v. Pembroke Corporation* (1912), 76 J.P. 365.

[2] In the case of a private sewer, the person draining thereto must have a right, acquired by grant or prescription, to drain thereto. Because a particular sewer is a public sewer, it does not follow that a particular person must have a right to drain into it, if he can only get access thereto through private land, and this point is therefore covered by the ensuing words of the section: *see* s. 37 (3).

[3] 1936 Act, s. 37 (4).

[4] *Princes Investments Ltd. v. Frimley and Camberley U.D.C.* [1962] 2 All E.R. 104.

[5] *I.e.*, s. 25 of the 1875 Act: *see Woodford U.D.C. v. Stark* (1902), 66 J.P. 536.

ing (or each separate premises), and to reject plans providing for drainage in combination, at least where there is an existing sewer available. This is not provided for in as many words in section 37 (3), but it seems to follow from the wording of section 38 (1),[1] and the authority are, under section 37 (3), apparently entitled only to insist on the drain being made to "connect with a sewer" (which, it is submitted, must mean "connect directly"), or to "discharge into a cesspool"; plans providing for combined drainage terminating in a cesspool, if otherwise unexceptional, would therefore, it seems comply with section 37 (3).[2]

Whenever separate drainage could be insisted upon for each of two or more buildings, to be made to communicate with an existing sewer,[3] the authority may as an alternative require the buildings to be drained in combination into the existing sewer, by means of a private sewer (which under the Public Health Acts Amendment Act, 1890, section 19, would have been described as a "single private drain"), to be constructed by the owners to the directions of the authority, or (at the option of the authority), by the authority on behalf of the owners.[4]

This power may be exercised subject to the following:—

(1) It must appear to the authority that the buildings in question may be drained more economically or advantageously in combination;

---

[1] "Where a local authority might under the last preceding section require each of two or more buildings to be drained separately into an existing sewer . . ."

[2] The drain may also be made to discharge into "some other place", such as a soakaway.

[3] If the sewer was constructed before 1937, this must be a public sewer. If it is a private sewer, there must be an easement or some other right to connect to it, as the authority's requirement cannot here override private rights: see, *e.g. Wood* v. *Ealing Tenants Ltd.* [1907] 2 K.B. 390.

[4] 1936 Act, s. 38 (1).

(2) Combined drainage cannot be insisted upon, except by agreement with the owners of the buildings concerned, in respect of "any building for the drainage of which plans have been previously passed by the authority";

(3) Combined drainage cannot be insisted upon otherwise than "when the drains of the buildings are first laid";

(4) The proportions in which the expenses of constructing, maintaining and repairing the communicating private sewer are to be borne by the owners concerned, must be fixed by the authority. The authority must give notice of their decision on such a matter to each owner affected,[1] and any owner aggrieved may appeal to the local magistrates' court.[2]

(5) Any sewer constructed by the local authority under this provision is not to be deemed to have become a public sewer as a consequence of such construction.[3]

(iii) *Appeals*. Facilities are given by sections 37 (2), 37 (3), 37 (4), and 38 (1), for a person aggrieved by a decision of the local authority under the provisions hereinbefore discussed, to appeal to the magistrates' court. Appeal in each such case will be by way of complaint for an order,[4] and the normal procedure of the Magistrates' Courts Act, 1980, will then apply. From the decision of the magistrates, either party will be able to appeal to the Crown court, under section 301 of the 1936 Act, as amended by the Courts Act,

---

[1] The notice must be in writing, signed by the authorised officer of the authority, and duly served, in accordance with ss. 283 to 285 of the 1936 Act: Shaw's Form PN 17 is appropriate.

[2] 1936 Act, s. 38 (2).

[3] *Ibid*, s. 38 (3), and compare s. 20 (1) (*b*), Chap. 2, *ante*, p. 24.

[4] 1936 Act, s. 300 (1); proceedings must be commenced within 21 days, *ibid.*, s. 300 (2).

1971. Alternatively, either party may appeal to the Queen's Bench Divisional Court on a case stated on a point of law.[1]

(c) Enforcement of Control.

This control, effected through the Building Regulations, 1976, can be enforced by the following means:

(i) The execution of work without submission of plans, where such are required, the execution of work otherwise than in accordance with the deposited plans, and the execution of work which contravene the Building Regulations, are made offences by s. 4 (6) of the Public Health Act, 1961, and proceedings may be taken in respect thereof;

(ii) Where work to which the Regulations apply is executed either without plans having been deposited, or notwithstanding the rejection of plans, or otherwise than in accordance with the deposited plans, and such work is of the description referred to in section 37 of the 1936 Act,[2] the authority may[3] by notice[4] to the building owner require him to pull down or remove the work, or, at his election, to comply with the authority's requirements.[5] If the owner in question fails to comply with

---

[1] Magistrates' Courts Act, 1980, s. 111; and *post*, Chap. 11, p. 180.

[2] Or various other sections of the Act, such as s. 25 (*see* Chap. 5, *ante*, p. 82), and others not the concern of this book.

[3] *See* 1936 Act, s. 65 (2); they have a discretion.

[4] This notice must be in writing, signed by the authorised officer of the authority, and duly served (1936 Act, ss. 283 to 285). Shaw's Forms BR 21 and BR22 are appropriate.

[5] These must be requirements which the authority might have made under s. 37 as "a condition of passing plans". Strictly speaking, there is no provision made in s. 37 for "conditional approvals", and s. 65 (2), here referred to, must be read as contemplating a rejection of the plans, coupled with an intimation to the effect that if certain amendments are made in the plans, they would be passed under the terms of the section.

such a notice within 28 days,[1] the authority may themselves act in default, and recover their expenses reasonably incurred[2] from him.[3] No notice may be issued under this section after the expiration of 12 months from the completion of the work in question, or if the plans had been passed by the authority, or not rejected within the "prescribed period[4]".

(iii) An action may be brought for an injuction for the alteration or removal of any work which offends against the Building Regulations. This action may be brought in the High Court, at the suit of the Attorney-General (on the relation of an interested person), or of a person aggrieved. In any such case, the court on granting the injunction, may, where the plans had been passed by the local authority, or notice of rejection of plans had not been given within the "prescribed period[1]", order the local authority to pay compensation to the owner of the work.[5]

4.   THE IMPROVEMENT OF EXISTING DRAINS.

Apart altogether from the question of nuisances and "unsatisfactory" drains, considered hereafter,[6] the

---

[1] Or such longer period as the magistrates' court may on his application allow.

[2] A reasonable sum by way of establishment expenses may be included: Local Government Act, 1974, s. 36.

[3] 1936 Act, s. 65 (2). The authority's expenses hereunder will be recoverable as a civil debt under s. 58 of the Magistrates' Courts Act, 1980, or alternatively as a simple contract debt in the local County Court, or the High Court (1936 Act, s. 294). The expenses will also be a charge on the property, being recoverable from the owner thereof, and should be registered in the local land charges register (see 1936 Act, s. 290, and Chap. 11, post, p. 176).

[4] Five weeks or such extended period as may be agreed: 1936 Act, s. 64 (4), as amended.

[5] 1936 Act, s. 65 (5). If the court proposes to make such an order against the local authority, it must first make the authority a party to the proceedings, if they are not already a party (ibid).

[6] Post, p. 136.

water authority or the local authority may take certain action to secure the improvement of existing private drains—at their expense. Further, where a private individual proposes himself to alter an existing drainage system, the local authority can exercise control over such work.

(a) 1936 Act, section 42.

Under this section, a water authority may, at their expense, close any existing drain or sewer[1] which communicates with a public sewer or a cesspool,[2] and fill up any such cesspool, and do any work necessary for these purposes. This power is exercisable only subject to the following:

(i) The drain or sewer in question, though sufficient for the effectual drainage of the premises,[3] must either be "not adapted to the general sewerage system of the district,[4]" or, in the opinion of the authority, "otherwise objectionable";

(ii) Before exercising the power to close the existing drain, etc., the authority must first provide in a position "equally convenient to the owner of the premises, a drain or sewer equally effectual for the drainage thereof and communicating with a public sewer[5]";

[1] The expression is here clearly intended to refer to private sewers only; the alteration, closure, etc., of public sewers could be effected under s. 22 of the 1936 Act (*ante*, p. 20); therefore s. 14 (5) of the Water Act, 1973 (requiring consultation with the local authority) does not apply here.

[2] *See* definition in s. 90 (1).

[3] If the drainage is not so sufficient, action could normally be taken under s. 39; *infra*, p. 138.

[4] It is not clear what is meant here by the term "district"; it does not seem that the area of the authority is necessarily intended.

[5] Substituted drainage communicating immediately with a cesspool does not, therefore, comply with the section.

(iii) Notice[1] of the authority's proposals must be given to the owner of the premises in question, and, if he is aggrieved as regards either the position or the sufficiency[2] of the drain or sewer proposed to be provided by the authority, he may appeal to the local magistrates' court.[3]

(b) 1936 Act, section 41.

This section, which applies throughout a local authority's district,[4] prohibits the repair, reconstruction or alteration of the course of any underground[5] drain which communicates with a sewer,[6] cesspool or any other receptacle for drainage, without giving to the local authority[7] at least 24 hours' notice[8] of an intention to do so. This prohibition does not apply to the following:

(i) A case of emergency; but in any such case, the prohibition applies to the covering over of the drain or sewer in question;

(ii) Drains or sewers constructed by, or belonging to, the British Railways Board, or which run under, across, or along a railway;

(iii) Drains or sewers constructed by or belonging to docks undertakers, so far as such are situate in or on land of the undertakers used for the purposes of the undertaking.

---

[1] Such notice must be in writing, signed by the authorised officer of the authority, and duly served (1936 Act, ss.283 to 285); Shaw's Form PH 60 is appropriate.
[2] But not on other grounds.
[3] He may appeal from the decision of the magistrates to the Crown court: 1936 Act, s. 301; Courts Act, 1971.
[4] Local Government Act, 1972, Schedule 14, para. 4.
[5] Note the limitation of the operation of the section.
[6] Not necessarily a public sewer; but even a private sewer must itself drain into a public sewer or a receptacle for drainage.
[7] **Not** the water authority in this case.
[8] This must be in writing and duly served (*see* 1936 Act, ss. 283 and 285).

(c) 1961 Act, sections 19 and 29.

Where the use of a drain is being discontinued, the local authority may require it to be disconnected and sealed at such points as they may specify,[1] and if a building is being demolished, a notice[2] served by the authority may require the person undertaking the demolition (*inter alia*) to disconnect and seal, at such points as the proper officer of the authority may reasonably require, any sewer or drain in or under the building, and/or to remove any such sewer or drain and seal any sewer or drain with which the sewer or drain to be removed is connected.[3]

5. UNSATISFACTORY DRAINS.

The Acts of 1936 and 1961 vest several distinct powers in local authorities which enable them to deal with drains or private sewers that are unsatisfactory in one respect or another. These powers overlap to some extent, but it seems that the authority have a discretion in selecting which procedure to follow and section 18 of the 1961 Act ("power to repair") is expressly conferred without prejudice to the powers contained in section 39 of the 1936 Act.[4] The most specific of these is section 40 of the 1936 Act, dealing with the condition of certain pipes and appurtenances to drains. Section 39 deals with cases where satisfactory provision has not been made for the drainage of a buildng, and the nuisance clauses of the Act (sections 92 to 100), which are not confined in their operation to buildings, provide a residuary control whereby nuisances in drains may be abated. There is also a summary power given by section 17 of the 1961 Act to remedy stopped up drains, which is of great use in practice. In addition, a local authority may act as contractor, on the application of the owner

---

[1] 1961 Act, section 19, and *see ante*, page 55.
[2] In writing; Shaw's Form PN. 82 is appropriate.
[3] 1961 Act, section 29.
[4] *Ibid*, section 18 (6).

or occupier of premises, to cleanse or repair drains, waterclosets, sinks or gullies.[1] The other powers will now be considered in detail.

(a) Ventilation, etc., of Drains.

Section 40 of the 1936 Act specifies three particular requirements which must be observed, and provides that if it appears to the local authority that on any premises there is a contravention of the section, they may by notice[2] require the owner or the occupier of the premises to execute such work as may be necessary to remedy the defect; in default of compliance therewith, the local authority *or* the water authority may do the work themselves, and recover the expenses reasonably incurred[3] by them from the person in default.[4]

The requirements specified in the section are as follows:

"(i) No pipe for conveying rain water from a roof shall be used for the purpose of conveying the soil or drainage from any sanitary convenience[4];

(ii) The soil pipe from every watercloset[5] shall be properly ventilated;

(iii) No pipe for conveying surface water[6] from

---

[1] 1961 Act, section 22.

[2] This notice must be in writing, signed by the authorised officer of the authority, and duly served (*see* 1936 Act, ss. 283 to 285). Shaw's Form PH 15 is appropriate.

[3] A reasonable sum by way of establishment expenses may be added to these: Local Government Act 1974, s. 36.

[4] 1936 Act, s. 40 (4), as amended by the Water Act 1973, Schedule 8, para. 38, and s. 290 (6). The expenses will be recoverable summarily as a civil debt under s. 58 of the Magistrates' Courts Act, 1980, or by simple action in the county court or the High Court (1936 Act, s. 294). If the owner of the premises is the party charged, it seems that the expenses will be a charge on the premises (1936 Act, s. 291 (1)), and should, therefore, be registered in the local land charges register. *See also* Chap. 11, *post* p. 176.

[5] Defined in s. 90 (1), and *see post*, Chap. 10, p. 153.

[6] This expression includes "water from roofs": 1936 Act, s. 90 (1).

any premises shall be permited to act as a
ventilating shaft to any drain or sewer carrying foul water.[1]"

(b) Satisfactory Provision for Drainage.

Section 39 of the 1936 Act is a more general section,
enabling the local authority to require (*inter alia*) satisfactory provision to be made for the drainage of an
existing building. The control is exercised in manner
similar to that applicable to section 40 of the Act, in
that the authority must serve a notice,[2] and may then
act themselves in default of compliance therewith, and
recover their expenses in so acting from the party in
default.[3] Only the owner[4] of the premises may be required to make satisfactory provision for drainage, but
either the owner or the occupier[5] may be required to
take the other action referred to in the section. It
should also be noted that the section applies only to
buildings,[6] and not to all types of premises.[7]

Action may be taken by the local authority under
the section whenever the authority consider that in the
case of a building:

"(*a*) satisfactory provision[8] has not been, and

---

[1] This expression is not defined in the Act.

[2] *See* note [2], on p. 137; Shaw's Form PN 23D is appropriate.

[3] *See* note [4], on p. 137.

[4] As defined by s. 343 (1) of the 1936 Act: Chap. 11, *post*, p. 186.

[5] The local authority have a discretion in selecting the appropriate party,
but they must take into consideration the rights and duties as between the
owner and the occupier, where appropriate: *Croydon Corporation v. Thomas*, [1947] K.B. 386.

[6] *See ante*; p. 126.

[7] As defined by s. 343 (1) of the 1936 Act.

[8] This expression is not expressly defined in the section, except that it is
provided that subsections (3) and (4) of s. 37 (*supra*, p. 128) shall apply to
the present section (*see* subsection (2) thereof). If the drains are sufficient,
the authority cannot use the present section to secure an improvement
therein at the expense of the owner of the premises. If the authority decide
to alter a private system of drainage, they may do so under s. 42 of the
1936 Act, or if they wish to alter their own sewerage system they may do
so under s. 22, *ibid.*, but in either case any consequential alterations to
private drains or sewers will have to be executed at the expense of the
authority (*supra*, p. 134, and *St. Martin's-in-the-Fields Vestry v. Ward*,
[1897] 1 Q.B. 40).

ought to be, made for drainage as defined in section 37 of this Act[1]; or

(b) any cesspool,[2] private sewer, drain, soil pipe, rain water pipe, spout, sink or other necessary appliance provided for the building, is insufficient or, in the case of a private sewer or drain communicating directly or indirectly with a public sewer, is so defective as to admit subsoil water; or

(c) any cesspool[3] or other such work or appliance as aforesaid provided for the building is in such a condition as to be prejudicial to health[4] or a nuisance[5]; or

(d) any cesspool,[3] private sewer or drain formerly used for the drainage of the building, but no longer used therefor, is prejudicial to health[4] or a nuisance.[5]"

Paragraphs (a) and (b) of this subsection cannot be invoked in respect of any building which belongs to statutory undertakers[6] and which is held or used by them for the purposes of their undertaking, other than houses,[7] or buildings used as offices or showrooms which do not form part of a railway station.[8]

---

[1] The conveyance of rain water from roofs is included in this expression: *ante*, p. 138.

[2] *See* definition in s. 90 (1) of the 1936 Act, and *post*, p. 152.

[3] *See* definition in s. 90 (1) of the 1936 Act, and *post*, p. 152.

[4] *I.e.*, "injurious, or likely to cause injury, to health": 1936 Act, s. 343 (1).

[5] *Post*, page 141.

[6] *See* definition in s. 343 (1) of the 1936 Act.

[7] *I.e.*, "dwelling-houses, whether private dwellinghouses or not": 1936 Act, s. 343 (1).

[8] It seems that a house which forms part of a railway station is outside this special exemption, and subject to the control afforded by the section. *See* s. 39 (3), and proviso thereto.

(c) Power to Repair.

Section 18 of the 1961 Act[1] provides that where it appears to a local authority that a drain or private sewer is not sufficiently maintained and kept in good repair and can be sufficiently repaired at a cost not exceeding £50, the authority may, after giving not less than seven days notice[2] to the person or persons concerned,[3] cause the drain or sewer to be repaired; the authority may thus take the remedial action themselves, without having to follow the more dilatory procedure of s. 39 of the 1936 Act, under which they must first serve a notice and wait for the person on whom the notice is served to default. The expenses of the authority incurred under the section are recoverable[4] from the person concerned, to a maximum of £50; further, if the expenses are not in excess of £2, the authority may remit and not attempt to recover them.

(d) The Nuisance Clauses.

A detailed discussion of the provisions of the 1936 Act dealing with statutory nuisances (sections 92 to 100 inclusive) would be out of place in the present work, but it should be appreciated that action may be taken under these provisions in a proper case, to secure the abatement of a nuisance in a private sewer or drain, or a cesspool or any other appliance used in connection with a private drainage system. No action can, however, be taken under these provisions in respect of a

---

[1] In this Part of the 1961 Act all the definitions of Part II of the 1936 Act will apply: 1961 Act, s. 1 (1).

[2] This must be in writing, signed by the authorised officer and duly served: 1936 Act, ss. 283–5, Shaw's form PN. 76 is appropriate.

[3] *See* s. 18 (5) of the 1961 Act.

[4] The expenses may be apportioned by the local authority. In proceedings for recovery of expenses the court must inquire whether the drain or sewer was in fact not sufficiently maintained and kept in good repair; and if the court considers that the authority were not justified in so concluding, the authority will not be able to recover the expenses (s. 18 (3)).

public sewer or sewage works vested in the local authority.[1]

Statutory nuisances may exist as a consequence of a variety of causes; those of importance for present purposes include "premises[2] in such a state as to be prejudicial to health or a nuisance", and "any accumulation or deposit which is prejudicial to health or a nuisance".[3]

"Prejudicial to health" is defined in s. 343 (1) of the 1936 Act as meaning "injurious, or likely to cause injury to health", and if this can be established, it is not necessary to establish a nuisance as well. It is now clear that "nuisance" in this context is to be given its ordinary common law meaning as either a *public* nuisance (to Her Majesty's subjects as such) or a *private* nuisance, which latter involves two properties; the defendant's, where the cause arises, and the plaintiff's, which suffers the nuisance, inconvenience, etc.[4]

Where a statutory nuisance is alleged to exist, and the authority are so satisfied, it is their duty to serve an abatement notice[5] on the person "by whose act, default, or sufferance the nuisance arises or continues, or, if that person cannot be found, on the owner or occupier of the premises on which the nuisance arises.[6]" If default is made in compliance with the abatement notice, the authority cannot themselves forthwith act in default (as is the case with a notice served under section 39 or section 40), but must first make a complaint to a justice of the peace, and a summons will

[1] *R. v. Parlby* (1889), 22 Q.B.D. 520, and *Fulham Vestry v. London CC.,* [1897] 2 Q.B. 76.
[2] This expression is defined by s. 343 (1) of the 1936 Act to include "messuages, buildings, lands, casements and hereditaments of any tenure".
[3] 1936 Act, s. 92 (1) (*a*) and (*c*).
[4] *Betts v. Penge U.D.C.* [1942] 2 K.B. 154, read with *National Coal Board v. Neath B.C.* [1976] 2 All E.R. 478.
[5] The notice must be in writing, signed by the authorised officer of the authority and duly served: *see* 1936 Act, ss. 283 to 285. Shaw's form PH 106A is appropriate.
[6] 1936 Act, s. 93.

then be issued requiring the defendant to appear before the local magistrates' court.[1] The court then have power to make a "nuisance order", and the authority will be able to act themselves in default of compliance with such nuisance order, and recover their expenses in so doing from the person in default.[2]

It will be observed that this procedure is more advantageous to the local authority in one respect, in that a decision as to the legality of the proceedings is obtained from the court before the authority has acted in default and expended ratepayers' money on a private individual's premises. On the other hand, where proceedings are taken under section 39, default action will have to be taken first, and the legality of the authority's proceedings will be tested normally only after money has been expended,[3] and in proceedings taken to recover such moneys from the party charged. Action under section 39 will, however, normally be more expeditious than nuisance proceedings.

(e) Stopped up drains.

Section 17 of the 1961 Act[4] gives a power to a local authority to require[5] the owner or occupier of premises on which a drain, private sewer, watercloset or soil pipe is stopped up, to remedy the defect within 48 hours. In default, the local authority[6] may carry out the work themselves and recover the expenses from the

---

[1] *Ibid.*, s. 94.

[2] If the owner of the premises is the party charged, the expenses will be a charge on the property and should be registered in the local land charges register; *see* 1936 Act, ss. 95 and 96. A reasonable sum by way of establishment charges may be added to the expenses actually incurred: Local Government Act 1974, s. 36.

[3] The recipient of a notice under s. 39 may appeal to the court: *see* s. 290 (7) and 300 (2). This does not, however, occur frequently in practice.

[4] As amended by the Local Government Act, 1972, Schedule 14, para. 36. The power may, however, be delegated to a named officer by virtue of s. 101 of the 1972 Act.

[5] By notice in writing duly signed and served in accordance with ss. 283–5 of the 1936 Act. Shaw's Form PN. 75 is appropriate.

[6] Or an officer, if this power also has been delegated.

person in default; they may, however, remit any of such expenses that do not exceed £2. Once again, as in the case of action under s. 18, this power may be exercised without prejudice to action under s. 39 of the 1936 Act.[1]

(f) Improper Construction or Repair.

If a watercloset, drain or soil pipe is so constructed or repaired as to be prejudicial to health[2] or a nuisance,[3] the person who undertook or executed the construction or repair will be liable to prosecution for an offence, unless he can show the prejudice to health or nuisance could not have been avoided by the exercise of reasonable care.[4]

6. LOAN OF CONVENIENCES.

In any case where work is being carried out at premises by a local authority or by the owner or occupier in pursuance of a requirement under s. 39 of the 1936 Act,[5] the local authority may supply on loan any temporary sanitary conveniences required in substitution for any watercloset or other sanitary convenience disconnected as a consequence of the work.[6] Such a loan may be made only at the request of the occupier of the premises; the conveniences may be used free of charge for the first seven days, but the authority are entitled to make a charge for supplying, removing and cleansing any conveniences lent for more than seven days. If the works are necessary because of some defect in a public sewer, no charge at all may be made under the section.

---

[1] Section 17 (4).
[2] *See* 1936 Act, s. 343 (1).
[3] *Ante* p. 141.
[4] 1961 Act, s. 20.
[5] Above, page 138.
[6] 1961 Act, s. 23.

7.   PRIVATE IMPROVEMENTS.

Whether the local authority initiate action towards securing some improved method of drainage for an existing dwelling, or the private owner decides to carry out improvements without waiting for any "prodding" from the local authority, the law may entitle him, in certain circumstances, to some measure of financial assistance. Thus:

    (*a*) If he is carrying out improvements, as distinct from "ordinary repairs", he may be able to obtain an improvement grant towards the cost from the local housing authority[1];

    (*b*) If he proposes to instal a watercloset in a dwelling not already so equipped, for the exclusive use of the occupants, he may be able to obtain an "intermediate grant" from the local housing authority[2];

    (*c*) If he proposes to convert a privy or earthcloset, etc., to a watercloset, he may be able to obtain a contribution from the local authority[3];

    (*d*) If the rent of the dwelling is controlled under the Rent Act,[4] he may be able to increase the rent payable by his tenant.[5] If the rent is regis-

---

[1] Housing Act, 1974, Part VII. The maximum amount that may be paid by way of grant is £5,000: Circ. 86/77 of the Department of the Environment.

[2] Housing Act 1974, Part VII. The maximum amount of such a grant for this purpose is £350: *ibid.*

[3] Act of 1936, s. 47; *post*, Chap. 10, p. 166.

[4] Rent Act, 1977, Sched. 3, apart from the cases where there has been an improvement grant, a tenancy will be controlled if the rateable value of the premises does not exceed £30 (outside London) and if the tenancy was subsisting on 6th June, 1957: *ibid.*, s. 17.

[5] The maximum amount of the increase will normally be twelve and a half *per cent, per annum* of the amount expended by the landlord: Rent Act, 1977 s. 32. If the improvements to the drainage system in question were carried out as part of private street works executed under Part XI of the Highways Act, 1980 (or some local Act), the amount of such expenditure falling on the landlord will rank as "improvements" for these purposes: Rent Act, 1977, s. 34.

tered under the Act, no such increases can be made.[1]

8. THE DRAINAGE OF TRADE PREMISES.

The drainage of trade premises is regulated by the Public Health (Drainage to Trade Premises) Act, 1937 (as amended by the Public Health Act, 1961, and the Control of Pollution Act, 1974), which by section 14 (2) thereof, is to be construed as one with the 1936 Act; every part of each Act must therefore be construed as if contained in one Act, "unless there is some manifest discrepancy which makes it necessary to hold that the later Act has modified the earlier[2]". It is here proposed first to discuss the definitions contained in the Act, then the circumstances in which trade effluent may be discharged into public sewers,[3] and the special machinery provisions of the statute.

(a) Definitions.

Trade effluent is defined in section 14 (1) of the Act of 1937[4] as meaning "any liquid, either with or without particles of matter in suspension therein, which is wholly or in part produced in the course of any trade or industry carried on at trade premises, and, in relation to any trade premises, means any such liquid as aforesaid which is so produced in the course of any trade or industry carried on at those premises, but does not include domestic sewage". All laundry effluent that comes within the definition is now subject to the control

---

[1] Rent Act, 1977, s. 45.

[2] *Maxwell on the Interpretation of Statutes*, 11th edn., p. 33.

[3] The discharge of trade effluent direct into "streams" is regulated by the Control of Pollution Act, 1974, discussed *ante*, Chap. 8, p. 109. The discharge of such effluent direct into the sea is not regulated by statute, but at common law the person discharging any matter into the sea will be responsible for any nuisance thereby caused (*Hobart v. Southend-on-Sea Corporation* (1906), 75 L.J.K.B. 305).

[4] There is a slightly different definition for the purposes of the Control of Pollution Act, 1974.

of the Act.[1] "Domestic sewage" is not defined under either the 1937 or the 1936 Act, and it is, presumably intended to be understood in much the same sense as water supplied for "domestic purposes" in the Waterworks Clauses Act, 1847.[2]

To understand this expression it is also necessary to appreciate the definition of "trade premises". By the same section of the 1937 Act it is provided that " 'trade premises' means any premises used or intended to be used for carrying on any trade or industry", but it does not define "trade" or "industry", and these words must therefore be given their ordinary dictionary meanings. Under the 1961 Act[3] and the Control of Pollution Act, 1974,[4] an extended definition is given to this expression so as to include premises used (in whole or in part and whether for profit or not) for agricultural or horticultural purposes, or for scientific research or experiment. Effluent from a farm is therefore now to be treated as trade effluent.

(b) The discharge of trade effluent.

Section 1 of the 1937 Act as amended by the Water Act 1973, provides that, notwithstanding the terms of section 34 of the 1936 Act[5], the occupier of any trade premises may discharge into the water authority's public sewers any trade effluent proceeding from those premises. (i) in certain circumstances, without the water authority's express consent, and in all other cases, (ii) subject to the prior consent of the authority having been obtained. Further, paragraphs (a) and (b)

---

[1] The exemption formerly contained in s. 4 (4) of the 1937 Act has been abolished by the repeal of this subsection (and s. 65 of the 1961 Act) by Schedule 9 of the Water Act, 1973.

[2] "If the purpose is one for which, according to the ordinary habits of domestic life, people require water in their houses, the purpose is a domestic purpose": *per* Atkinson, J., in *re Willesden Corporation and Municipal Mutual Insurance Ltd.'s Arbitration*, [1944] 2 All E.R. 600, at p. 602.

[3] Section 63.

[4] Section 105 (1).

[5] *Ante*, p. 118.

of section 27 (1) of the 1936 Act[1] do not apply to trade
effluent which may lawfully be discharged into a public
sewer by virtue of this statute.[2]

(i) *"Deemed" Consent.*

Trade effluent may not now be discharged without
consent, even if the discharge is made pursuant to an
agreement made prior to, and still subsisting, at the
time of the passing of the 1937 Act. The exemptions
formerly provided for by s. 4 of the 1937 Act have now
all been withdrawn as a result of repeals of s. 4 (4) by
the Water Act 1973 and of s. 4 (1), (2) and (3) by the
Control of Pollution Act, 1974. Agreements previously
safeguarded by s. 7 (4) of the 1937 Act will now not be
exempt from the need to obtain consent to a discharge,
by virtue of section 43 of the 1974 Act. However, in
cases formerly covered by such exemptions, the owner
of premises concerned may obtain a "deemed consent"
by serving a notice on the water authority under s. 43
(2); but this deemed consent may then be cancelled
and an actual consent (subject, perhaps, to new conditions as to charges, etc.) may be substituted therefor.

(ii) *Discharge with express Consent.*

Normally the consent of the water authority must be
obtained under the 1937 Act to the discharge of trade
effluent from trade premises into public sewers.

(1) Applications for consent do not have to be
made in as many words, but it is an offence
to discharge any trade effluent,[3] otherwise than
in accordance with a "trade effluent notice[4]"

---

[1] *Ante*, Chap. 5, p. 58.
[2] *See* s. 1 (2) of the 1937 Act.
[3] If the particular trade effluent is not covered by the 1937 Act, it should
be remembered that an offence may be committed under s. 27 (1) of the
1936 Act (*ante*), p. 88).
[4] This must specify the nature or composition of the effluent, the maximum quantity to be discharged in any one day, and the highest rate of
discharge of the effluent. The notice must be served in accordance with s.
95 of the 1974 Act; Shaw's Form TP 5 is appropriate.

served on the water authority by the owner or occupier of the premises, and before the expiration of the "initial period[1]". Any such notice is to be treated as an application for the consent of the authority to discharge the effluent named therein.[2]

(2) When the water authority receive a trade effluent notice, they are no longer obliged to send a copy of the notice to any "interested body", and the interested body no longer has a suspensory veto on any further action.[3]

(3) Having received such a notice, the authority may, at any time within the initial period,[4] direct that no effluent shall be discharged until a specified date after the expiration of the initial period. The authority may either give consent unconditionally, or subject to such conditions as they may think fit with respect to any of the following matters:

(a) the sewer or sewers (or any altered drain or sewer[5]) into which the effluent may be discharged, the nature and composition of the effluent, the maximum quantity that may be discharged on any one day, and the highest permissible rate of discharge[6];

(b) the period or periods of the day during which the trade effluent may be discharged from the trade premises into the sewer;

---

[1] A period of two months, or such less time as may be agreed to by the water authority, from the day on which the trade effluent notice is served on the authority: s. 2 (1).
[2] See s. 2 (2).
[3] But in an appropriate case they will presumably inform a harbour or conservancy authority. Section 2 (4) was repealed by the Act of 1974.
[4] See footnote [1] above.
[5] 1974 Act, s. 43 (6), subject to regulations.
[6] 1937 Act, s. 2 (3).

(*c*) the exclusion from the trade effluent of all condensing water;

(*d*) the elimination or diminution of any specified constituent of the trade effluent, before it enters the sewer, where the local authority are satisfied that the constituent would, either alone or in combination with any other matter with which it is likely to come into contact while passing through any sewers—

   (i) injure or obstruct those sewers, or make specially difficult or expensive the treatment or disposal of the sewage from those sewers, or

   (ii) (where the trade effluent is to be, or is, discharged into a sewer having an outfall into any harbour or tidal water or into a sewer which connects directly or indirectly with a sewer or sewage disposal works having such an outfall) cause or tend to cause injury or obstruction to the navigation on, or the use of, the said harbour or tidal water;

(*e*) the temperature of the trade effluent at the time when it is discharged into the sewer, and acidity or alkalinity at that time;

(*f*) the payment by the occupier of the trade premises to the local authority of charges for the reception of the trade effluent into the sewer, and for the disposal thereof, regard being had to the nature and composition and to the volume and rate of discharge of the trade effluent so discharged, to any additional expense incurred or likely to be incurred by a sewerage authority[1] in connection with the reception or disposal of the trade effluent, and to any revenue likely to be derived by a sewerage authority from the trade effluent;

(g) the provision and maintenance of such an inspection chamber or manhole as will enable a person readily to take at any time samples of what is passing into the sewer from the trade premises; and

(h) the provision and maintenance of such meters as may be required to measure the volume and rate of discharge of any trade effluent being discharged from the trade premises into the sewer, and for the testing of such meters.[2]

These powers, it will be noted are wide (and see also s. 59(2)), but conditions may not be imposed outside these provisions. Moreover, conditions may at any time be varied by a direction given by the local authority under s. 60 of the 1961 Act as amended by s. 44 of the 1974 Act. Notice of any such direction must be given, and the owner or occupier of trade premises affected has a right of appeal to the Secretary of State against a direction. Once a direction has been given under the section, no further direction may normally be given for a period of two years.[3]

---

[1] Defined in s. 90 (1) of the 1936 Act; see s. 14 (2) of the 1937 Act.
[2] See section 59 of the 1961 Act, which replaces the power contained in s. 5 of the 1937 Act to make byelaws regulating similar matters.
[3] Section 60 (2) of the 1961 Act; but see s. 45 of the Control of Pollution Act 1974.

(c) Special machinery of the 1937 Act.

In addition to the provisions above discussed, the Act of 1937 enables water authorities to enter into agreements with the owner or the occupier of trade premises for the reception and disposal of any trade effluent produced on those premises.[1] A section is included enabling the water authority to obtain certain information,[2] and to take samples of trade effluents.[3] The 1937 Act provides that "nothing in this Act shall affect any right with respect to water in a river, stream or watercourse, or authorise any infringement of such a right"[4]; but it should also be noted that the Act must be read with the 1936 Act, in particular, in this context, with section 30 thereof.[5]

There are elaborate provisions for the Secretary of State to determine questions under the Acts of 1937 and 1974, and any such decision will be final on questions of fact.[6]

---

[1] *See* s. 7 (1) of the 1937 Act. For a precedent of such an agreement, *see* (1961) 25 Conv. N.S., 38 and 662.
[2] Section 9, *ibid.*, and s. 93 of the Control of Pollution Act, 1974.
[3] Section 10 of the 1937 Act, as amended by s. 67 (3) of the 1961 Act, and Schedule 3 of the 1974 Act.
[4] 1937 Act, s. 13.
[5] *Ante*, Chap. 8, p. 111.
[6] 1937 Act, s. 3; 1974 Act, s. 45 (4).

CHAPTER 10

SANITARY CONVENIENCES

1. INTRODUCTORY.

Statutory provisions regulating the installation, maintenance, etc., of sanitary conveniences are to be found in several Acts of Parliament, of which the most important is the Act of 1936, while certain specific classes of buildings are affected in this respect by other statutes. These provisions are enforceable by the local authority, not the water authority. In the first place, it is important to appreciate the specialised meanings of particular words, as used by Parliament in the 1936 Act. These definitions apply, to the most part, only for the purposes of Part II of that Act.[1]

By section 90 (1) of the 1936 Act, the words listed below are in Part II of that Act (unless the context otherwise requires) to have the meanings respectively assigned to them:

" 'cesspool' includes a settlement tank or other tank for the reception or disposal of foul matter from buildings;

'closet' includes privy;

'earthcloset' means a closet having a movable receptacle[2] for the reception of faecal matter and

---

[1] Except in so far as hereinafter mentioned. Many of the definitions of the 1936 Act have been extended to the 1961 Act: see s. 1 thereof. These definitions will also apply to the Building Regulations 1976 made under ss. 61–70 of the 1936 Act, as amended by the Health and Safety at Work, etc., Act, 1974.

[2] An earthcloset having a fixed receptacle will, therefore, be a mere privy for the purposes of the statute.

its deodorisation by the use of earth, ashes or chemicals,[1] or by other methods;

'sanitary conveniences' means closets and urinals;

'watercloset' means a closet which has a separate fixed receptacle connected to a drainage system and separate provision for flushing from a supply of clean water[2] either by the operation of mechanism or by automatic action."

The question sometimes arises in practice whether "closet" in these definitions is intended to refer only to the sanitary apparatus itself, or whether it includes the room, shed or outhouse in which the apparatus is housed. This is a question to be determined according to the context in which the term is used; thus, in the phrase "sufficient closet accommodation[3]", a reference to the apparatus alone is presumably intended, but in the reference to closets which are "prejudicial to health or a nuisance[4]", it seems that the shed, etc., in which the apparatus is housed is to be included in the term "closet[5]".

In several places in the pages which follow, we shall have occasion to refer to a requirement of the Act of 1936, to the effect that a building must have a sewer "available". Section 90 (6) provides that there shall not be deemed to be a sewer available, **unless**:

"(*a*) there is within 100 feet of the site[6] of the building or proposed building, and at a level

---

[1] The usual type of chemical closet is therefore an "earthcloset".

[2] A slop closet is thus not a "watercloset".

[3] *See* s. 44 (1) (*a*) and (*aa*), *post*, p. 157.

[4] *See* s. 44 (1) (*b*), and s. 45 (1), *post*, pp. 157 and 159.

[5] It is submitted that the primary meaning of "closet", which is not displaced by any of the statutory definitions set out above, is that of a small room or retiring chamber, and that the word should be used or understood in the more specialised sense as referring to the sanitary apparatus, only where the context clearly shows that such was the intention of the legislature.

[6] *See* Chap. 9, *ante*, p. 128.

which makes it reasonably practicable to construct a drain to communicate therewith, a public sewer or other sewer which the owner of the building or proposed building is, or will be, entitled to use, **and**

(b) the intervening land is land through which he is entitled to construct a drain;
and [the building or proposed building] shall not be deemed to have a sufficient water supply available unless it has a sufficient supply of water laid on, or unless such a supply can be laid on to it from a point within 100 feet of the site of the building or proposed building, and the intervening land is land through which the owner of the building or proposed building is, or will be, entitled to lay a communication pipe:

Provided that, for the purposes of this definition, the limit of 100 feet shall not apply, if the local authority undertake to bear so much of the expenses reasonably incurred in constructing, and in maintaining and repairing, a drain to communicate with a sewer or, as the case may be, in laying and in maintaining and repairing, a pipe for the purpose of obtaining a supply of water, as may be attributable to the fact that the distance of the sewer, or of the point from which a supply of water can be laid on, exceeds 100 feet."

2. SANITARY ACCOMMODATION FOR NEW BUILDINGS.

The local authority's powers to ensure that sufficient and satisfactory closet accommodation is to be provided for a new building[1] are, by virtue of section 43 of the 1936 Act, made dependent on Building Regulations, 1976[2]. When plans for a building[3] or an extension of a building are deposited under the Regulations, the local authority **must** reject the plans, unless:

(*a*) the plans show that "sufficient and satisfactory" closet accommodation, consisting of one or more waterclosets[4] or earthclosets[4] will be provided, **and**, if the plans show that the building is likely to be used as a workplace, factory or workshop[5] in which people of both sexes will be employed or in attendance,[6] that sufficient and satisfactory closet accommodation for persons of each sex will be provided; **or**

(*b*) that they (the authority) may properly dispense with such provision.

An appeal lies, on the application of the person depositing the plans, to the local magistrates' court against a decision of the local authority under this section, on any of the following (but no other[7]) questions:

(i) whether the provision of accommodation may properly be dispensed with;

(ii) whether the accommodation proposed is sufficient and satisfactory; or

(iii) whether the provision of an earthcloset

---

[1] Note that the section is not confined in its operation to houses.

[2] For a discussion of the extent of this control, *see* Chap. 9, *ante*, p. 126.

[3] *See* definition of this term, *ante*, p. 126.

[4] As defined in s. 90 (1); *ante*, p. 153.

[5] "Factory" and "workshop" are to be defined as used in the Factories Act, 1961 (*post*, p. 161); "workplace" is defined in s. 343 (1) of the 1936 Act; *post*, p. 160.

[6] For an example of circumstances in which persons may be "in attendance", but not employed at a place, *see Bennett v. Harding*, [1900] 2 Q.B. 397.

[7] *See* 1936 Act, s. 43 (2).

should, in a particular instance, be approved in lieu of a water-closet.

The words "sufficient and satisfactory" are not defined for the purposes of this section, and the question seems to be mainly one of fact. Under a predecessor of the present section, it was held that the provision of a separate closet or privy for every house could not be insisted upon,[1] but at the present day, it is doubtful whether a court would quash a requirement of the local authority under this section for every house to be provided with separate accommodation; on the other hand, the authority could certainly not require separate accommodation to be provided for every type of building to which the section applies.[2]

It is specifically provided in the section that the authority may not reject the plans merely on the ground that "the proposed accommodation consists of or includes an earthcloset or earthclosets", unless a sufficient water supply and sewer are available.[3]

Each case under the section must be considered on its merits, and not in accordance with pre-conceived general principles for which there is no express statutory justification,[4] and it seems that the local authority cannot require any particular type of sanitary accommodation to be provided, where that proposed is both sufficient and satisfactory.[5]

---

[1] *Clutton Union v. Ponting* (1879), 4 Q.B.D. 340.
[2] Such as, *e.g.* a lock-up shop or office in close proximity to public conveniences.
[3] *See* explanation of this term in s. 90 (6), *supra*, p. 153.
[4] *Wood v. Widnes Corporation*, [1898] 1 Q.B. 463.
[5] *Robinson v. Sunderland Corporation* (1898), 78 L.T. 194, but compare *Carlton Main Colliery v. Hemsworth R.D.C.*, [1922] 2 Ch. 609.

3. SANITARY ACCOMMODATION FOR EXISTING BUILDINGS.

(a) Buildings other than special[1] buildings.

(i) *Section* 44 *of the* 1936 *Act.* Under this section, as amended by s. 21 of the 1961 Act, if it appears to the local authority:

"(a) that any building[2] is without sufficient[3] close accommodation; or

(aa) that any part of a building,[2] being a part which is occupied as a separate dwelling,[4] is without sufficient[6] closet accommodation; or

(b) that any closets provided for or in connection with a building are in such a state as to be prejudicial to health[5] or a nuisance[6] and cannot without reconstruction be put into a satisfactory condition,"

the authority are under a duty to serve a notice[7] on the owner of the building requiring him to provide such closets, additional closets or substituted closets as may be necessary, the closets in any such case to be either earthclosets or waterclosets. In the special case of a building consisting of several dwellings (case (aa)), the owner of the building may appeal to a court on the

---

[1] *See* para. (b), below, as to the sense in which the term "special buildings" is here used, as referring to shops, factories, workshops and workplaces, etc.

[2] Other than a factory, workshop, workplace or shop (as to which *see* page 160, *post*): s. 44 (3).

[3] *See* comment on this term in para. 2, *supra*.

[4] It would seem that "separate" in this context means distinct as a dwelling, not necessarily separated physically or partitioned off; *see* further in Woodfall on Landlord and Tenant, 26th edition, at page 1105.

[5] *I.e.*, "injurious, or likely to cause injury, to health": 1936 Act, s. 343 (1).

[6] As to the significance of this expression, see *ante*, page 141.

[7] The notice must be in writing, signed by the authorised officer of the authority, and duly served (*see* ss. 283 to 285 of the 1936 Act). Shaw's Form PH 67 is appropriate.

ground that he has a cause of action in respect of the occupation of part of the building as a separate dwelling (*e.g.*, because it offends against a covenant against sub-letting in a lease) and that the need for the works to be executed would not arise but for that occupation.[1]

The local authority cannot, under this section, require the abolition of a privy, unless it is either insufficient or a nuisance, etc., and a watercloset cannot be required (except in substitution for an existing watercloset) to be provided, unless a sufficient water supply and sewer are available.[2] It also seems that the authority cannot require a particular type of watercloset (or earthcloset) to be provided, if that proposed falls within the statutory definition.[3]

It will also be noted that this section can only be used in respect of nuisances, where the closet in question cannot be rendered satisfactory without reconstruction; if the closet[4] in question is capable of repair, the powers of section 45 (discussed below) should be used. It may be important, therefore in a particular case, to decide whether a closet is or is not capable of repair. Unfortunately, there is no rule of thumb or standard to be applied in answering such a question (similar, for example, to section 4 of the Housing Act, 1957). In the law of landlord and tenant, repair has been said to include the replacement of parts, but not the renewal of the whole, and new work which is an exact replacement of the old is none the less capable of being "reconstruction", as distinct from repair.[5]

Paragraph (*aa*) of this sub-section deals with the case

---

[1] Public Health Act, 1961, s. 21 (2).
[2] *See* definition of this expression in s. 90 (6) of the Act; *supra*, p. 153.
[3] *See* p. 153, *supra*, and *Robinson v. Sunderland Corporation*, p. 156, *supra*.
[4] The term here probably includes the shed, etc., in which the sanitary apparatus is housed: *see* above, p. 153.
[5] *See, e.g., Agar v. Nokes* (1905), 93 L.T. 605, a case on the meaning of "reconstruction", as used in a local authority's building byelaws.

of houses occupied as two or more dwellings; in a case where a building is in "multiple occupation" it may be found necessary to use the powers of Part II of the Housing Act, 1961 in order that existing conveniences, etc., may be required to be maintained in a proper condition.[1]

If the notice of the authority is not complied with, the authority may themselves execute the work required, and recover their reasonable expenses[2] thereby incurred from the owner of the premises.[3]

(ii) *Repair of defective closets.* It is provided by section 45 of the 1936 Act that, if it appears to the local authority that any closets[1] provided for or in connection with a building[4] are in such a state as to be prejudicial to health or a nuisance,[5] but they can without reconstruction[6] be put into a satisfactory condition, the authority must[7] serve a notice[8] on the owner or the occupier[9] of the building, requiring him to execute such steps[10] or execute such works as may be necessary.

In so far as the notice requires work to be executed, in any case of default in compliance therewith, the authority may themselves execute the work required, and recover their reasonable expenses[11] thereby in-

---

[1] And *see* the Housing (Management of Houses in Multiple Occupation) Regulations, 1962, S.I., 1962, No. 668.

[2] A reasonable sum by way of establishment espenses may be included in this sum: Local Government Act 1974, s. 36.

[3] 1936 Act, s. 44 (2), and s. 290, and *post*, Chap. 11, p. 176.

[4] Other than a shop, factory, workshop, or workplace: s. 45 (4).

[5] *See* notes [5] and [6] on p. 157, *supra*.

[6] *See* the discussion of this expression in para. (i), *supra*.

[7] The authority are under a duty to take such action.

[8] The notice must be in writing, signed by the authorised officer of the authority, and duly served (*see* ss. 283 to 285 of the 1936 Act). Shaw's form PN 20 is appropriate.

[9] The authority must select the person responsible as between the owner and the occupier: *see Croydon Corporation v. Thomas*, [1947] K B. 386, decided under s. 75 (dustbins).

[10] "By cleansing the closets or otherwise". Presumably "otherwise" must here be construed as being *ejusdem generis* with "cleansing".

[11] *See* note [2] above.

curred, from the person in default.[1] In so far as the notice requires steps other than the execution of works to be undertaken, any person required to take such steps is liable to a fine in the event of non-compliance with the terms of the notice.[2]

(b) Special buildings.

(i) *Houses*. The extent to which a particular house may be defective in the matter of sanitary conveniences, is a matter to be taken into consideration when deciding whether or not the house is unfit for human habitation for any of the several purposes of the Housing Act, 1957 (*see* section 4 (1) thereof). A special application of this principle is also to be found in the case of houses occupied by members of more than one family (1957 Act, section 36 and section 78), and as to houses in "multiple occupation", see Housing Act, 1961.[3]

(ii) *Workplaces*. By section 46 of the 1936 Act, every building used as a "workplace[4]" must be provided with sufficient and satisfactory accommodation in the way of sanitary conveniences,[5] and provision must also be made (where necessary) for persons of each sex.[6] In the event of the local authority being satisfied that this

---

[1] 1936 Act, s. 45 (2), and s. 290, and *post*, Chap. 11, p. 176.

[2] *Ibid.*, s. 45 (3). In any such proceedings the defendant is entitled to question the reasonableness of the requirements of the local authority, or their decision to serve the notice on him and not the owner, or the occupier (as the case may be).

[3] As amended by the Housing Act, 1969; *ante*, p. 159.

[4] This expression is defined in s. 343 (1) of the 1936 Act. It "does not include a factory or workshop, but save as aforesaid includes any place in which persons are employed otherwise than in domestic service". It will be noticed that the present section applies only to such workplaces as are buildings (and not being shops: s. 46 (4)), and that the reference to factories and workshops in the original section was deleted by the Factories Act, 1937, but see now s. 175 of the Factories Act, 1961. In *Bennet v. Harding*, [1900] 2 Q.B. 397, a stable yard for London cabbies was held to be a workplace within the meaning of the predecessor of the present section.

[5] This term includes urinals: *see* definition, *supra*, p. 153.

[6] Regard must be had to the number of persons employed in, or in attendance at, the building.

requirement is not being complied with in respect to a particular building, they must by notice[1] require the owner or the occupier of the building "to make such alterations in the existing conveniences, and to provide such additional conveniences, as may be necessary".

If the notice of the authority is not complied with, the authority may themselves execute the work required, and recover their reasonable expenses[2] thereby incurred from the person in default.[3]

(iii) *Factories and Workshops.* The Factories Act, 1961, makes no distinction between a factory and a workshop, but provides[4] that any reference in any other legislation to a factory or workshop within the meaning of the Factory and Workshop Acts, 1901 to 1929 (repealed by the Factories Act, 1937, itself now replaced by the Factories Act, 1961), shall be construed as references to a factory within the meaning of that Act of 1961. Section 175 of the Act of 1961 gives an extended definition of "factory", which it would be outside the scope of this work to set out[5]; suffice it here to state that in general, a factory means premises in which persons are employed in manual labour.[6]

By section 7 of the Factories Act, 1961 (which is one of the sections of that Act enforceable by the local authority[7]), it is provided that "sufficient and suitable

---

[1] The notice must be in writing, signed by the authorised officer of the authority and duly served (*see* ss. 283 to 285 of the 1936 Act). Shaw's Form PH 46 is appropriate.
[2] *See post*, p. 176.
[3] *See* 1936 Act, s. 46 (3) and s. 290, and *post*, Chap. 11, p. 176.
[4] By s. 184 (1) thereof; and *cf*. s. 343 (1) of the 1936 Act.
[5] *See, e.g.*, Lumley's Public Health, 12th edition, Vol. 3, p. 3215, or *Redgrave's* "Factories, Truck and Shops Acts".
[6] In any particular case, reference should be made to the terms of the section which is particularly complicated.
[7] *See* s. 8 (1) of the 1961 Act.

sanitary conveniences[1] for the persons employed in the factory shall be provided, maintained and kept clean, and effective provision shall be made for lighting them and, where persons of both sexes are or are intended to be employed (except in the case of factories where the only persons employed are members of the same family[2] dwelling there), the conveniences shall afford proper separate accommodation for persons of each sex". As he is empowered to do[3], the Home Secretary has made regulations[4] determining what is "sufficient and suitable provision" for the purposes of the section; in particular, these regulations provide for a minimum number of conveniences, according to the number of persons employed in the factory. It should be noted that compliance with the regulations seems to amount to compliance with the terms of the section, provided that the conveniences are kept clean and effectively lighted.[5]

Under section 1 of the 1961 Act (which is also normally enforceable by the local authority[6]), the walls of sanitary conveniences in factories must be kept clean

---

[1] "Sanitary conveniences" is defined by s. 176 to include "urinals, water-closets, earthclosets, privies, ashpits, and any similar convenience". The local authority cannot, under either the section itself, or the Regulations referred to below, insist on any particular type of sanitary convenience being provided.

[2] This term is not defined in the Act, but for the purposes of the Rent Acts, has been widely construed (see, e.g., Price v. Gould (1930), 143 L.T. 333, and Brock v. Wollams, [1949] 2 All E.R. 715).

[3] By s. 7 (2).

[4] The Sanitary Accommodation Regulations, 1938 (S.R. & O. 1938. No. 611), and also the specialised Railway Running Sheds (No. 1) Regulations, 1961 (S.I., 1961, No. 1251). Running sheds, falling within the definition of a factory for the purposes of the 1961 Act, are excluded from "railway premises" for the purposes of the Offices, Shops and Railway Premises Act, 1963 (post, p. 163) by s. 85 (1) thereof.

[5] See art. 9 of the Regulations of 1938. It should also be noted that neither the section nor the Regulations require the sanitary accommodation in question to be provided within the curtilage of the factory, provided it is "conveniently accessible" to the persons employed.

[6] But not invariably; see, e.g., the Local Authorities (Transfer of Enforcement) Order, 1938 (S.R. & O. 1938, No. 488), made by the Home Secretary under s. 8 (2).

and lime washed[1] and the whole of the factory must be kept clean and free from effluvia arising from any drain, sanitary convenience or nuisance.

Contraventions of any of these provisions are made offences under the Act of 1961,[2] and the local authority may take proceedings against the person responsible[3] in the local magistrates' court.[4]

(iv) *Shops and Offices.* A "shop" is not expressly defined in the 1936 Act, but all "shops" are now excluded from the operation of ss. 44, 45 and 46 of the 1936 Act,[5] and not only those to which the Shops Act 1950 applies.

By s. 9 of the Offices, Shops and Railway Premises Act, 1963, there must be provided at all premises to which the Act applies, at places conveniently accessible to the persons employed to work in the premises, suitable and sufficient sanitary accommodation[6] for their use. Conveniences so provided must be kept clean and properly maintained, and effective provision must be made for lighting them. Standards as to what is meant by "suitable and sufficient" for this purpose have been laid down in Regulations made by the former Minister of Labour under this section.[7]

The section applies to shops, offices and railway premises, all of which are elaborately defined in section 1; and there are exemptions for cases where only the employers' relatives or outworkers work at the prem-

---

[1] This requirement applies to all factories; *see* the Factories (Cleanliness of Walls and Ceilings) Order, 1960 (S.I., 1960, No. 1794).

[2] *See* s. 155.

[3] Usually the occupier of the factory, except in the case of tenement factories, when the owner will usually be liable (*see* sections 121 and 122).

[4] *See* s. 164. An appeal lies at the instance of any person aggrieved at the decision of the magistrates to the Crown court; *see* s. 165 of the 1961 Act.

[5] Offices, Shops and Railway Premises Act, 1963, s. 9 (6).

[6] Not defined for the purpose of this section.

[7] The Sanitary Conveniences Regulations 1964, S.I., 1964, No. 966. *See* also the special exemption provided for in s. 9 (5) of the Act.

ises (s. 2) and where only 21 man hours weekly are normally worked (s. 3).

(v) *Food Premises*. Premises of the type hereinafter discussed may also be shops, in which case they will be subject to the provisions of the Offices, Shops and Railway Premises Act, 1963; otherwise, if they are not so subject and they form part of a building, they will be subject, in addition to the provisions mentioned below, to the normal provisions of section 44 and 45 of the 1936 Act.

The Food Hygiene (General) Regulations, 1970,[1] made under section 13 of the Food and Drugs Act, 1955, make detailed provisions for the observance of hygiene and cleanly practices at "food premises", *i.e.*, premises on or from which there is carried on any "food business[2]". Sanitary conveniences[3] at such premises must be kept clean and in efficient order and no room which contains a sanitary convenience may be used as a food room.[4] Detailed provisions for the observance of cleanly practices at slaughterhouses are contained in the Slaughterhouses (Hygiene) Regulations, 1958.[5]

These various regulations are enforceable by the local authority,[6] and in the event of any contravention of these requirements, proceedings for an offence under the Act may be taken against any person carrying on a food business.[7] In an extreme case the court may

---

[1] S.I., 1970, No. 1172.

[2] As defined in regulation 3.

[3] Defined in regulation 2 to mean "a water closet, urinal, chemical closet or similar convenience".

[4] Regulation 16 (3). As to similar provisions in relation to markets, *see* the Food Hygiene (Markets, Stalls and Delivery Vehicles) Regulations, 1966, S.I., 1966, No. 791, reg. 14. *See* also the Food Hygiene (Docks, Carriers, etc.) Regulations, 1960 (S.I., 1960, No. 1602), reg. 15.

[5] S.I., 1958, No. 2168, and *see* the Slaughterhouses Act, 1974.

[6] 1955 Act, s. 87 (2); and *see* definition of "local authority" in s. 85, *ibid*.

[7] Regulation 33; a food handler also may sometimes be responsible: reg. 33 (1).

make an order closing the premises under the Food and Drugs (Control of Food Premises) Act, 1976.

Milk is expressly excluded from the definition of "food" in these Regulations, for dairies are subject to their own code of Regulations,[1] made under the Food and Drugs Act, 1955. Sanitary accommodation is not separately regulated under these regulations, and many dairies will come within the provisions relating to shops, above discussed, but it is provided[2] that "No person shall use as a milking house, milk room or for the handling, processing or storage of milk, any building or part of a building, which is so situated or constructed as to give rise to the risk of contamination of the milk". Except inso far as the same relates to dairy farms, this provision is enforceable by the local sanitary authority,[3] and a contravention thereof is punishable summarily.[4]

(vi) *Places of Entertainment.* Section 20 of the Local Government (Miscellaneous Provisions) Act, 1976, replacing s. 89 of the 1936 Act, enables a local authority to require the occupier of a "relevant place" to provide sanitary appliances[5] as may be specified by the authority, and to make them available for public use, free of charge (if so required). A "relevant place" for this purpose means any place (including a building) normally used for public entertainment or exhibitions, or for the sale of food or drink to members of the public, or any place occasionally used for any of those purposes or as a betting office.

(vii) *Theatres and Cinemas.* Licences for the use of premises for the public performance of plays may be

---

[1] The Milk and Dairies (General) Regulations, 1959, S.I. 1959. No. 277.
[2] *See* art. 11 (1) of the Regulations.
[3] *See* art. 3 (*b*) of the Regulations.
[4] *See* art. 34, *ibid.*
[5] This means water closets, other closets, urinals and washbasins: s. 20 (8).

granted by district councils under the Theatres Act, 1968 (as amended by s. 204 of the Local Government Act 1972), and restrictions may be specified therein on any topic (which presumably could include the provision of public conveniences) except as to the nature of the plays or the manner of performing plays presented at the premises.[1]

Cinematograph licences also are issued by district councils under the Cinematograph Acts, 1909 and 1952, but it does not seem that the licensing authority have any powers to impose conditions as to sanitary conveniences.[2]

(viii) *Agricultural units*.[3] A sanitary authority may by notice require the "appropriate person"[4] to provide suitable and sufficient sanitary conveniences available for the use of workers employed in agriculture, at any "agricultural unit"[5] where such conveniences are lacking. Fixed equipment may be required for such a case only if special circumstances exist.[6] and any person aggrieved by such a notice may appeal to the local magistrates' court within 28 days from the service of the notice.[7] Failing such appeal, non-compliance with the notice is punishable as an offence under the section.

4.   THE REPLACEMENT OF EXISTING CLOSETS.

Under section 47 of the 1936 Act, provided the building has a sufficient water supply and sewer available,[8]

---

[1] Theatres Act, 1968, s. 1 (2) and First Schedule.
[2] *See* Home Office Circular 150/1955.
[3] Agriculture (Safety, Health and Welfare Provisions) Act, 1956, s. 3; *see* also ss. 4 and 5, *ibid*.
[4] The landlord or occupier of the unit; *see* s. 3 (6).
[5] "Land occupied as a unit for agricultural purposes": 1956 Act, s. 24 (1).
[6] *Ibid*, s. 3 (5).
[7] *Ibid*, s. 3 (7).
[8] *See* definition in s. 90 (6) of the 1936 Act, *supra*, p. 153.

the local authority may[1] by notice[2] require the owner of a building to replace any closets,[3] other than waterclosets,[4] provided for, or in connection with, the building, by waterclosets, or alternatively require the owner to permit the local authority to execute such works of replacement.

This power may be exercised even where the closets are not insufficient in number or prejudicial to health or a nuisance,[5] but if the owner executes the work himself he is entitled to recover one-half of the expenses reasonably incurred by him in the execution thereof, from the local authority. Similarly, where the authority themselves execute the work, they may recover from the owner an amount not exceeding one-half of their reasonable expenses incurred in the execution thereof.[6]

The authority's expenses, in so far as they are recoverable as above mentioned, will be recoverable summarily, or as a civil debt, and will be a charge on the property,[7] but in any legal proceedings, the necessity of the works cannot be called into question.[8]

---

[1] This power is optional, not a mandatory duty similar to those imposed by ss. 44 and 45.

[2] The notice must be in writing, signed by the authorised officer of the authority, and duly served (see ss. 283 to 285 of the 1936 Act). Shaw's Form PH 11A is appropriate. The form of notice must state the effect of subsection (3): see s. 47 (2).

[3] See definition in s. 90 (1), supra, p. 153.

[4] In any such case action should be taken under s. 45, supra.

[5] Ante, p. 141.

[6] See s. 47 (3). Similarly, where the owner of a building, on his own initiative, and without receiving any notice from the local authority, proposes to provide a watercloset for the building in substitution for a closet of some other type, the authority may (if they think fit) agree to bear half his expenses incurred in such replacement (see s. 47 (4)). In this case there need not be a water supply and sewer "available".

[7] Section 47 (5) and s. 290, and see post, Chap. 11, p. 176.

[8] Section 47 (5).

5. SUPPLEMENTARY PROVISIONS.

Sections 48 to 52 (inclusive) of the Act of 1936 contain certain supplementary provisions on the subject matter of this chapter.

(a) Overflowing and Leaking Cesspools.[1]

If the contents of any cesspool[2] soak therefrom or overflow, the local authority **or** the water authority may by notice[3] require the person responsible to execute such works, or take such steps (by periodically emptying the cesspool or otherwise) as may be necessary for preventing the soakage or overflow.[4]

In so far as the notice served under this section requires work to be executed, in any case of default of compliance therewith, the authority may themselves execute the work required, and may recover their reasonable expenses[5] thereby incurred from the person in default.[6] In so far as the notice requires steps other than the execution of works to be undertaken, any person required to take such steps is liable to a fine in the event of non-compliance with the terms of the notice.[7]

(b) Offences.

The following matters are specifically made offences under the Act:

> (i) The occupation of any room, or the permit-

---

[1] 1936 Act, s. 50, as amended by the Water Act, 1973, Schedule 8, para. 40.

[2] *See* definition in s. 90 (1), *supra*, p. 152.

[3] This must be in writing, signed by the authorised officer of the authority, and duly served (*see* ss. 283 to 285 of the 1936 Act). Shaw's Form PN 23 is appropriate.

[4] The subsection does not, however, apply to the effluent from a properly constructed tank, if the effluent is of such a character, and is so carried away and disposed of, as not to be prejudicial to health or a nuisance.

[5] A reasonable sum by way of establishment expenses may be added to this figure: *see* Local Government Act 1974, s. 36.

[6] *See* s. 50 (2) and s. 290, and *post*, Chap. 11, p. 176.

[7] *See* s. 50 (3).

ting of such room to be occupied, in contravention of section 49 (1), after seven days' notice[1] from the local authority prohibiting such occupation.

This section provides that a "room which or any part of which, is immediately over a closet,[2] other than a watercloset or earthcloset,[2] or immediately over a cesspool,[2] midden or ashpit,[3] shall not be occuped as a living room, sleeping room or workroom".

(ii) Failing to cause the flushing apparatus of a watercloset[2] to be kept supplied with water sufficient for flushing, or where necessary, to be properly protected against frost, or in the case of an earthcloset,[2] failing to cause it to be kept supplied with dry earth or other suitable deodorising material.[4]

The only person who may be charged with an offence under this provision is the occupier of the building[5] in, or in connection with, which the closet in question is provided.

Sometimes the facts of a particular case may fall within both this section and section 45, but it is suggested that in such a case the machinery of this section should be used.

(iii) Where a sanitary convenience is used in common by the members of two or more families,[6] there may be an offence[7] if:

---

[1] This notice must be in writing, signed by the authorised officer of the authority, and duly served (*see* ss. 283 to 285 of the 1936 Act).

[2] *See* definition in s. 90 (1), *supra*, p. 153.

[3] These expression are not defined in the Act.

[4] *See* s. 51.

[5] The section applies to all types of buildings, shops, factories, etc., not being excluded.

[6] *See* note [2] on page 162, *supra*.

[7] Section 52.

(a) any person injures or improperly fouls the convenience, or anything used in connection therewith, or wilfully or by negligence causes an obstruction in the drain[1] therefrom[2]; or

(b) the convenience, or the approach thereto, is, for want of proper cleansing or attention, in such a condition as to be insanitary; in any such case such of the persons having the use thereof in common as are in default, or. in the absence of satisfactory proof as to which of them is in default, each of them, will be liable in respect thereof.[3]

(c) Power to examine drains, etc.

Section 48 of the 1936 Act as amended by the Act of 1973[4] gives the relevant authority power to examine the condition of a sanitary convenience,[4] drain, private sewer or cesspool,[5] to apply a test (other than a test by water under pressure), and to open the ground, if necessary for such purpose. Where the item concerned is a drain or private sewer connecting with a public sewer, the relevant authority is the water authority for the area, but in any other case, this will be the local authority.

A local authority may delegate this function (as in the case of other functions) to one of their officers.[6]

The power may be exercised only in certain circum-

---

[1] Obstruction of a sewer is not, apparently, an offence hereunder.
[2] The fine in respect of such an offence may not exceed £25. (1936 Act, s. 52, as amended by Criminal Law Act 1977, s. 31).
[3] Again the fine may not exceed £25, but there is a further fine not exceeding 25p for each day on which the offence continues after conviction. (ibid)
[4] 1973 Act, Sched. 8, para. 29.
[5] See definition in s. 90 (1), supra, p. 152.
[6] Section 101 of the Local Government Act 1972; s. 16 of the Public Health Act 1961 has been repealed by Sched. 30, ibid.

stances, where the authority (or possibly an officer of a local authority acting under delegated powers) consider there are reasonable grounds for believing that "the sanitary convenience, drain, private sewer or cesspool is in such a condition as to be prejudicial to health or a nuisance, or that a drain or private sewer communicating directly or indirectly with a public sewer is so defective as to admit subsoil water". The power will be enforceable by use of the right of entry given by section 287 of the Act,[1] but the authority must be careful to act (except by agreement with any landowner or other interested person) only within the powers of the section.

If the convenience or drain, etc., is found on examination to be in proper condition, the authority must, as soon as possible, reinstate any ground which has been opened and make good any damage done by them, and there is no provision made in the section enabling them to recover their expenses in so doing from any person. Even if the convenience or drain, etc., in question is found not to be in proper condition, their expenses incurred in the examination, etc., cannot be recovered.

---

[1] *See* Chap. 11, *post*, p. 175.

CHAPTER 11

PROCEDURE UNDER THE PUBLIC HEALTH ACTS

1. INTRODUCTORY.

Whilst it is not the object of this book to provide a commentary on all the many provisions of the Act of 1936, or to take the place, so far as public health legislation is concerned, of the standard works on the procedure in magistrates' courts,[1] it was considered desirable that a brief summary should be included of those procedural provisions of the 1936 Act which are common to the preceding chapters, and to which references has been made in the footnotes and the text.

Part II of the 1961 Act (concerned with Sanitation and Buildings) is to be "construed as one with Part II of the 1936 Act,[2] and therefore all the definitions of the latter Act will apply, as will the detailed procedural provisions. Part V (dealing with Trade Effluents) is to be construed as one with the Public Health (Drainage of Trade Premises) Act, 1937[3] as amended by the Public Health Act 1961, which must itself be construed as one with the Act of 1936, and also the Control of Pollution Act, 1974.[4] Most of the procedural provisions of the 1936 Act are contained in Part XII of that Act, and that Part applies equally to the sewerage powers of water authorities, as it does to the powers generally of local authorities.[5]

---

[1] Such, for example, as *Stone's* "Justices' Manual", to which reference should be made in any case of difficulty.
[2] 1961 Act, s. 1 (1).
[3] *Ibid.*, s. 1 (3).
[4] 1937 Act, s. 14 (2).
[5] Water Act 1973, s. 14 (2).

It is therefore proposed to deal first with the service of notices, and second with legal proceedings under the 1936 Act, interposing some comment on the ancillary powers of authorities which enable them to carry out their statutory functions.[1]

2. STATUTORY NOTICES.

Where the local or water authority are required to give a notice to a person under one or other of the sections of either of the Acts, this must be in writing,[2] and it must be signed by an officer of the authority who has been duly authorised in that behalf (either generally or specially) by the authority.[3] It will also be noticed that the notice is to be given by the **authority**. A local authority may arrange for any of their functions to be discharged by a committee, a sub-committee, one of their officers, or by another local authority.[4] This power has not been expressly extended to water authorities; although they may delegate functions to a committee,[5] there seems to be no power whereby they may delegate functions to one or more of their officials.[6]

Formal decisions of a local authority can be taken

---

[1] This term includes "powers and duties": s. 343 (1) of the 1936 Act.

[2] *See* s. 283 (1) of the 1936 Act. Section 95 of the Control of Pollution Act 1974 is to somewhat similar effect, but this applies only to the functions of water authorities under that Act.

[3] *See* s. 284 (1), and definition in s. 343 (1). A printed signature is sufficient: s. 284 (2), and so is a rubber stamp, provided it is affixed by an authorised officer: *Goodman v. J. Eban Ltd.*, [1954] 1 Q.B. 550, and *Plymouth City Corpn. v. Hurrell* [1967] 3 All E.R. 354.

[4] Local Government Act 1972, s. 101, but this does not, it is submitted, authorise delegation to a *single* member of the authority.

[5] Water Resources Act, 1963, Schedule 4, para. 11 (3), applied by s. 9 of the Water Act 1973.

[6] Unless s. 14 (2) be considered wide enough to confer such a power, in so far as sewerage functions under the 1936 Act are concerned. Otherwise the pre-1974 law relating to the local authorities will apply; *see* such cases as *Shoreditch Vesty v. Holmes* (1885), 50 J.P. 132, and *cf.*, in a somewhat different context, *Allingham v. Minister of Agriculture and Fisheries*, [1948] 1 All E.R. 780. Ratification *ex post facto* may, however, be sufficient: *Firth v. Staines*, [1897] 2 Q.B. 70; *Warwick R.D.C. v. Miller-Mead*, [1962] 1 All E.R. 212.

only by resolution of the Council,[1] and informal advice given by an official cannot bind the local authority as to the future action they may take.[2]

(a) Person to be served.

It is the duty of the authority to select the appropriate person on whom the notice is to be served. If the wrong person is served, he will be entitled to appeal as a "person aggrieved[3]", and the court may quash the notice.[4] Information as to the ownership, etc., of property may be obtained by serving a requisition for information,[5] and it is made an offence for any person on whom such a requisition may be served[6] either to fail to give such information, or knowingly to make a misstatement in respect thereof.[7]

(b) Methods of service.

The methods of service of notices are prescribed by section 285 of the 1936 Act,[8] and one of other of the methods there stated must be followed strictly (unless actual service can be proved to have been effected by some other means); however, subject to compliance with the terms of the section,[9] it seems that the authority

---

[1] Local Government Act, 1972, Schedule 12, para. 39.

[2] *Hodgson v. Southend-on-Sea Corporation*, [1961] 2 All E.R. 46; *Princes Investments Ltd. v. Frimley and Camberley U.D.C.*, [1962] 2 All E.R. 104.

[3] *See* s. 290 (3) (*e*) and (*f*), and *post*, p. 179.

[4] *Croydon Corporation v. Thomas*, [1947] K.B. 386. As to the meaning of "owner" *see* s. 343 (1), and *post*, p. 186.

[5] Shaw's Form PN 56 is useful for this purpose.

[6] Only the occupier of premises, or any person who either directly or indirectly receives rent in respect of the premises, may be asked to supply the required information, and the only information obtainable by this method is "the nature of his [the informant's] interest therein [the premises] and the name and address of any other person known to him as having an interest therein, whether as freeholder, mortgagee, lessee or otherwise".

[7] *See* 1936 Act, s. 277. Even if wrong information has been given as to ownership, a notice served in reliance on such false information may still be found to have been wrongly served: *Courtney-Southan v. Crawley U.D.C.*, [1967] 2 All E.R. 246 (a town planning case).

[8] As to the references in s. 285 to service by post, see section 7 of the Interpretation Act, 1978.

[9] For example, if the notice is to be affixed "to some conspicuous part of the premises", there must be no person thereon to whom it can be delivered.

are not bound to adopt any particular one of these
possible methods of service in any specific instance.[1]
The methods prescribed in this section apply equally
to a summons, as they do to other "documents" served
under the 1936 or 1961 Act.[2]

(c) Form of notice.

Apart from the requirement that the notice must be
in writing, and duly signed,[3] the notice need not follow
any particular form, as the Secretary of State has not
used his power to prescribe the forms to be used for
the purposes of the 1936 Act.[4] Nevertheless, the notice
should follow as nearly as practicable the wording of
the appropriate section, and the notice may be quashed
by the court if it is satisfied that there has been some
"informality, defect or error in, or in connection with,
the notice[5]", unless it is also satisfied that such error,
etc., was not a material one.[6] It is also important, where
the notice is one requiring the execution of works, that
the time within which the works are required to be
completed, should be reasonable,[7] and the nature of the
works required should be clearly stated.[8] Wheere there
is a right to appeal against the notice this must be
stated on the notice.[9]

3. POWER OF ENTRY.

A local or water authority may authorise in writing[10]
any of their officers to exercise the power of entry on

---

[1] *See Woodford U.D.C. V. Henwood* (1899). 64 J.P. 148.
[2] *See, e.g., R. v. Braithwaite*, [1918] 2 K.B. 319.
[3] *See* above, p. 173.
[4] *See* s. 283 (2).
[5] Section 290 (3) (*b*).
[6] Section 290 (4).
[7] Section 290 (3) (*d*).
[8] Section 290 (2); *Perry v. Garner*, [1953] 1 All E.R. 285.
[9] Section 47 (2) (*supra* , p. 167) requires the purport of that section also
to be set out. On the general principle, *see* s. 300 (3), and *Rayner v. Stepney
Corporation* [1911] 2 Ch. 312.
[10] *See* definition of "authorised officer" in s. 343 (1).

premises given by section 287 of the 1936 Act. Twenty-four hours' notice[1]—at least—must be given of the intentionn to exercise this power, and it may be exercised only at reasonable hours. The power is exercisable only for the purposes listed in the section,[2] and the officer exercising the power must, if required, produce a duly authenticated document showing his authority.

If the authorised officer is obstructed in endeavouring to exercise this power of entry, he may not use force, but must (if necessary) apply for a warrant to a justice of the peace, and if this warrant is issued, force, but only the minimum necessary, may then be used.[3]

4.   THE ENFORCEMENT OF STATUTORY NOTICES.

In most cases, notices served under the 1936 Act are enforceable by the authority, who are empowered to act themselves in default of compliance with the terms of the notice by the person on whom the notice is served; in a few cases,[4] the notice is enforceable only by means of proceedings taken against the person in default.[5]

(a) Recovery of expenses.

Where the local or water authority are authorised by either of the Acts of 1936 or 1961 to execute works in default of compliance with the terms of a statutory notice, it is commonly provided[6] that they may recover

---

[1] Except in the case of a factory or workplace: s. 287 (1), proviso. The notice must be in writing, signed and duly served: Shaw's Form PH 70 is appropriate.

[2] *See* s. 287 (1), and in particular, the power to enter "for the purpose of the performance by the council of their functions under this Act", or any byelaws made thereunder.

[3] *See* s. 287 (2); he must be able to show that the statutory procedure has been strictly observed: *Stroud v. Bradbury*, [1952] 2 All E.R. 76.

[4] *E.g.*, ss. 49, 51 and 52, Chap. 10, *ante*, p. 168.

[5] *See* below, p. 178.

[6] This applies to notices served under ss. 25, 39, 40, 44, 45, 46, 47, and 50 (and other sections with which this book is not concerned).

the expenses from the party in default.[1] These expenses must, however, have been reasonably incurred, and the work executed must not exceed that specified in the statutory notice. The expenses actually incurred may, however, be increased by a reasonable sum by way of establishment expenses.[2]

The expenses are recoverable by serving a demand,[3] and interest on the sum demanded will run as from the date of the demand.[4] The authority may also declare any sum so due to them to be repayable by instalments (with interest[5]), over a period not exceeding thirty years.[5]

Any sum which a local or water authority are entitled to recover under the Act may be recovered either as a civil debt in the local county court (unless the sum involved exceeds £750, in which case proceedings could be taken only in the High Court[6]), or summarily under section 58 of the Magistrates' Courts Act, 1980, before the local magistrates' court. If the proceedings are taken in the magistrates' court, the time limit is six months,[7] but it seems that in the county court this does not apply[8] and the ordinary six years for actions in contract applies.[9] In either case, the time runs from the service of the demand,[10] but there is no time limit

---

[1] *See* s. 290 (6). The liability of a mere agent or trustee is limited to the total amount of money he has in his hands on behalf of his principal: s. 294.

[2] Local Government Act, 1974, s. 36.

[3] This must be in writing, signed by the authorised officer of the authority, and duly served, in accordance with ss. 283 to 285, *supra*.

[4] Section 291 (3). The rate of interest may not at present exceed 7 per cent.: Public Health (Rate of Interest) Order, 1968, S.I. 1968, No. 231, made by the Minister under this section.

[5] Section 291 (2). For a form of order, *see* Shaw's Form PN 62.

[6] County Courts Act, 1959, s. 40, as amended by Administration of Justice Act, 1969, s. 1.

[7] Magistrates' Courts Act, 1980, s. 127.

[8] *Blackburn Corporation v. Sanderson*, [1902] 1 K.B. 794, distinguishing *Tottenham Local Board v. Rowell* (1876), 1 Ex. D. 514.

[9] Limitation Act, 1939, s. 2 (1).

[10] Section 293 (2).

within which the demand must be served, and it seems
that there is no reason why a fresh demand should not
be served at any time; certainly this is so where there
has been a change of owner.[1]

In cases where the person responsible for the payment of the authority's expenses is the owner of the
premises, those expenses become a charge on the property,[2] and the authority have all the powers and remedies given by section 121 of the Law of Property Act,
1925 (including a power of sale) for the enforcement
of such charge.[3] The charge should be registered in the
local land charges register,[4] but if the same is not so
registered, or if a charge is not disclosed on an official
certificate of the result of search, the charge will still
be enforceable against a purchaser of the land affected.
Any person who can prove he has suffered loss in
consequence, will be able to claim compensation from
the resigsration authority.[5] In any case the local authority could always demand payment of the expenses
from the "owner for the time being" of the premises[6].
These observations apply equally to expenses incurred
by a water authority under section 23 of the 1936 Act.

(b) Prosecutions.

In addition to specific offences created in the various
sections of the Acts of 1936 or 1961, the failure to
comply with a statutory notice to which section 290 of
the 1936 Act applies, is itself made an offence,[7] and in
addition to their right to execute works in default, the

---

[1] *Dennerley v. Prestwich U.D.C.* [1930] K.B. 1334.
[2] *See* s. 291 (1).
[3] The charge must be enforced within twelve years (Limitation Act 1939,
s. 4 (3)), of the date when the works were completed (*see Hornsey Local
Board v. Monarch Investment Building Society* (1889), 24 Q.B.D. 1).
[4] Maintained under the Local Land Charges Act 1975 (as amended). This
charge should be registered in Part II of the register (*see* the Local Land
Charges Rules, 1977).
[5] Local Land Charges Act 1975, s. 10.
[6] *See, e.g.*, s. 291 (2).
[7] By s. 290 (6).

authority may prosecute for an offence under the
section.

All offences under these statutes may be prosecuted
summarily,[1] but proceedings may be commenced only
by the local or water authority concerned, or by a
"party aggrieved[2]"; any other person who wishes to
commence proceedings may do so only with the written
consent of the Attorney-General.[3] Where a local or
water authority are taking proceedings, it must be
shown that the officer (or possibly, the member) who
lays the information in their name has been authorised
so to do either generally or specially.[4]

It may be considered appropriate in some prosecu-
tions to use the summary trial procedure of the Magistrates' Courts Act, 1980, which enables the accused
to plead guilty by post, thereby saving him time and
(much more important) making it possible for the prosecution to dispense in advance with the attendance of
witnesses in court. Where it is decided to use this
procedure, special documents, giving notice of the effect of section 12 of the 1980 Act, and summarising the
facts relating to the charge, in the prescribed forms,
have to be served upon the accused with the summons.
As none of the offences here considered are triable on
indictment, and usually are not punishable with a term
of imprisonment exceeding three months, the 1980 Act
procedure may be applied in any such case (*see* section
12 (1) thereof.). However, the authority may on occasion consider that the additional publicity that may
result from an oral hearing, is to be preferred to the
saving of time which results from the 1980 Act procedure; moreover, even when this procedure is used,

---

[1] Section 296.
[2] Section 298. For an illustration of the use of the term "party aggrieved"
in this context, *see, e.g., Sheffield Corporation v. Kitson*, [1929] 2 K.B. 322.
[3] As to the proof of any such consent having been given, see section 7 of
the Prosecution of Offences Act 1979.
[4] *Bob Keats Ltd. v. Farrant*, [1951] 1 All E.R. 899.

the accused may not wish to plead guilty, or if he does
he may prefer to attend court and explain his conduct
in person.

Where fines may be imposed for an offence under
the Acts discussed in this work, it should be noted that
the prescribed maxima may have been increased (in
many instances considerably) by the Control of Pollution Act, 1974, Schedule 2. The maximum fine under
section 290 (*b*) of the 1936 Act has been increased to
£500 by the Criminal Law Act 1977.

5.   APPEALS AND APPLICATIONS TO THE COURT.

Various sections of the 1936 Act provide for a person
aggrieved to appeal to the local magistrates' court
against a notice or other requirement of a local or
water authority given under the Act. In many cases
where the 1936 Act empowers a local authority to serve
a notice requiring action to be taken, it is also provided
that the provisions of Part XII of the Act shall apply
thereto,[1] and in that event a right of appeal is given by
section 290, and a number of grounds of appeal are
therein specified. In some cases further special grounds
of appeal are provided for in the particular section itse.[2]
Also in a number of cases,[3] the Act may provide for a
particular matter or question to be determined, in case
of dispute, by a magistrates' court. In any such case,
the proceedings are commenced by means of a complaint for an order, and the provisions of the Magistrates' Courts Act, 1980, will apply to such proceedings.[4] Once an appeal has been lodged against a notice,
the local authority cannot withdraw the notice without
the consent of the person(s) on whom it was served.[5]

---

[1] For example, ss. 25, 39 (1), 40, 44, 45, 46, 47, 50, etc., of the 1936 Act.
[2] For example, s. 21 (2) of the 1961 Act, amending s. 44 of the 1936 Act.
[3] *E.g.*, under s. 24 (3), *supra*, Chap. 5, p. 70.
[4] Section 300 (1).
[5] *Reg. v. Cannock Justices, ex parte Astbury* (1972), 70 L.G.R. 609.

In any case of an appeal, proceedings must be commenced within 21 days of the notice or determination, etc., appealed against,[1] but this time limit does not apply to an application to the court for them to determine a matter[2]; in the latter event the time limit of 6 months provided for in section 127 of the Magistrates' Courts Act, 1980, will be applicable.[3]

Unless the case is one which the parties might have referred to arbitration as an alternative to a reference to the court,[4] there is a right of appeal to the Crown court from the decision of the magistrates' court.[5] However, this right is given only to a "person aggrieved", and a local authority are not aggrieved (unless they have been ordered to pay costs) merely because a notice or order made by them has been quashed by the magistrates.[6] Alternatively, either party may ask the magistrates to state a case for the opinion of the High Court on a point of law,[7] and in the event of their refusing so to do, they may be ordered to state a case by an order in the nature of *mandamus*.[8] The Crown court also may be asked to state a case, but in a non-criminal matter, *mandamus* will not lie against them in the event of refusal.[8]

Where proceedings are taken in the county court (*e.g.*, for recovery of the authority's expenses as a simple contract debt), an appeal lies to the Court of Appeal on a point of law, in any case with leave, but if the amount involved exceeds £20, as of right (County Courts Act, 1959, section 108), and on a question of

---

[1] *See e.g.*, the several sections of the 1936 Act (*e.g.* s. 39 (1) incorporating s. 290 (3), and s. 300 (2).
[2] For example, under s. 35 (2): and *see* s. 300 (1) (*b*).
[3] *Nalder v. Ilford Corporation*, [1951] 1 K.B. 822.
[4] *See, e.g.*, s. 35 (2); where the matter is determined by arbitration, the Arbitration Act, 1950, will apply to the proceedings: *see* s. 31 (1) thereof.
[5] Section 301.
[6] *Jones v. Ealing Corporation*, [1959] 2 W.L.R. 194.
[7] Magistrates' Courts Act, 1980, s. 111.
[8] *R. v. Somerset Justices*, [1950] 1 All E.R. 264.

fact, as of right if the amount involved exceeds £200 (*ibid.*, section 109).

In any proceedings under the Act of 1936 or of 1961, a copy of a resolution of the authority concerned or of the appointment of, or of an authority given to, any officer of the authority, which is certified by the proper officer of the authority,[1] is admissible in evidence.[2]

Powers to appear in legal proceedings (either as plaintiffs or defendants) are given to a local authority by the Local Government Act, 1972, which also enable them to authorise one of their officers (or even one of their members) to conduct the proceedings on their behalf, although he may not be of counsel or a solicitor.[3]

6.   CLAIMS FOR COMPENSATION.

Under section 278 of the 1936 Act, a local or water authority must pay "full compensation" to any person who has sustained damage by reason of the exercise by the authority of any of their powers under the Act of 1936 or those provisions of the Act of 1961 incorporated therewith. This liability to pay compensation does not, however, apply in the following circumstances:

(*a*) Where the claimant himself has been in default.[4]

(*b*) In respect of action which the authority are under a duty to undertake, as distinct from a power. This is, however, to be construed strictly, and compensation is payable, for example, in respect of damage caused in the exercise of a power which is itself ancillary to a duty (*e.g.*, the power to lay a public sewer

---

[1] *Cf.* also para. 19 of Schedule 3 to the Water Act, 1973.
[2] Section 286.
[3] Local Government Act, 1972, ss. 222 and 223: and *see, ante,* p. 179.
[4] Sections 222 and 223; the latter section applies also to water authorities (*see* s. 223 (2) and s. 9 of the Water Act 1973).

through the claimant's land, in pursuance of the authority's duty to sewer their district under section 14).

(*c*) The right to claim under the section lies only where no action for damages can be brought.[1] Thus, if the authority lay a sewer through the claimant's land in a negligent manner, thereby causing special damage, he will have an action against them, and his remedy does not lie under this section.[2]

(*d*) No claim for compensation arises as a consequence of a declaration made under section 17 of the 1936 Act, vesting a sewer or any sewage disposal works in the authority.[3]

Any dispute as to the amount of compensation payable under this section is to be determined by arbitration,[4] unless the claim does not exceed £50, in which event, the matter may, on the application of either party, be referred to the local magistrates' court.[5] Where the claim for compensation is in respect of the construction of a sewer[6] in, on or over the claimant's land, the tribunal assessing the compensation must determine also "by what amount, if any, the value to the claimant of any land belonging to him has been enhanced by the construction of the sewer[7]".

---

[1] But no claim will lie in respect of acts lawful under the ordinary law apart from the statute: *see, e.g., Hall v. Bristol Corporation*, (1867) L.R. 2 C.P. 322.

[2] *Brine v. G.W. Rlwy. Co.* (1862), 2 B. & S. 402; *Clothier v. Webster* (1862), 6 L.T. 461.

[3] *See ante*, Chap. 4, p. 57, and s. 278 (3). The Secretary of State, on an appeal to him, may order compensation to be paid (s. 17 (3)).

[4] As prescribed by s. 303, below.

[5] Section 278 (2).

[6] Under s. 15; *ante*, Chap. 3, p. 35.

[7] Section 278 (4).

7. ARBITRATIONS.

Arbitrations generally under the 1936 Act will be conducted before a single arbitrator appointed by agreement between the parties, or, in default of agreement, by the Secretary of State.[1] In the case of claims in respect of damage involving the acquisition of land related to the laying of public sewers under section 15, however, the matter will fall to be determined by the Lands Tribunal, as the amount of the compensation is to be determined in accordance with the principles contained in the Land Compensation Act, 1961, replacing the former Acquisition of Land (Assessment of Compensation) Act, 1919.[2]

8. APPLICATIONS TO THE SECRETARY OF STATE.

Under section 322 of the 1936 Act, any person may complain to the Secretary of State to the effect that a local or water authority have failed to discharge their functions under the Act in any case where they ought to have done so; this is particularly appropriate where the authority have failed to carry out their duty to maintain a public sewer under section 23. The Secretary of State may then hold a local inquiry[3] and thereafter make an order declaring the authority to be in default, and directing them to discharge their functions.[4]

---

[1] 1936 Act, s. 303; any such arbitration will be subject to the Arbitration Act, 1950: s. 31 (1).

[2] Lands Tribunal Act, 1949, s. 1 (3).

[3] Section 250 of the Local Government Act, 1972, will apply to such an inquiry, and it will also be subject to the supervision of the Council on Tribunals by virtue of the Tribunals and Inquiries Act, 1971, and the Tribunals and Inquiries (Discretionary Inquiries) Order, 1975 (S.I. 1975, No. 1377). Any procedural rules for such inquiries would therefore be subject to s. 11 of the Tribunals and Inquiries Act, 1971.

[4] Act of 1936, s. 322 (2) and (3).

9. OTHER PROCEEDINGS.

In addition to proceedings provided for under the Act of 1936 or of 1961, a private individual may have other forms of redress against a local or water authority arising out of the exercise by them of their statutory functions. These may be summarised as follows[1]:

(*a*) Action for damages. This has already been discussed; the main points are that a water or local authority in the exercise of sewerage duties cannot plead the defence of non-feasance and they must not create a nuisance.[2]

(*b*) Action by the Attorney-General at the relation of a private individual for a declaration and/or an injunction. This may be brought where the authority are acting *ultra vires*; the remedy sought is discretionary and the plaintiff must have an interest in the matter. Where the claim is based on nuisance, a private individual may be able to sue for an injunction without joining the Attorney-General as a party, in circumstances where it can be shown that the plaintiff has sustained special damage.[3]

(*c*) Proceedings on an application for judicial review[4] of *certiorari* or prohibition, where it can be shown the authority have erred in law or have acted unfairly to the prejudice of the applicant, or *mandamus* to require them to perform a statutory duty. Cases where these

---

[1] On this subject *see* "Judicial Review of Administrative Action", 3rd edn., by S. A. de Smith.

[2] 1936 Act, s. 31.

[3] *See*, for example, *Cook v. Bath Corporation* (1868), L.R. 6 Eq. 177 (a highway case).

[4] Under Order 53 of the Rules of the Supreme Court.

will lie in the present context are exceptional,
but they may arise.[1]

10. THE MEANING OF "OWNER".

In many cases under the 1936 Act or the 1961 Act,
action falls to be taken by the water or local authority
against the "owner" of the premises concerned. It is,
therefore, of importance to appreciate the meaning of
this expression as used in the Acts of 1936 and 1961.

By section 343 (1) of the 1936 Act, "owner" is defined as meaning "the person for the time being receiving the rackrent of the premises in connection with
which the word is used, whether on his own account or
as agent or trustee[2] for any other person, or who would
so receive the same if those premises were let at a
rackrent". "Rackrent" is defined in the same section
to mean, in relation to any property, "a rent which is
not less than two-thirds of the rent at which the property might reasonably be expected to let from year to
year, free from all usual tenant's rates and taxes, and
tithe rent-charge (if any), and deducting therefrom the
probable average annual cost of the repairs, insurance
and other expenses (if any) necessary to maintain the
same in a state to command such rent[3]".

These definitions have been the subject of much case
law, which it is not the province of this book to discuss[4];
but the commonest case causing difficulty is where the
property is occupied by a tenant who holds from an
intermediate lessor. As a general rule (says Lumley[5])

---

[1] As to *mandamus, see* Chapter 3, *ante*, page 33.
[2] The right to recover expenses incurred by an authority against such an
"owner" is strictly limited: *see* note [1] on p. 177.
[3] This is to be computed with reference to conditions at the commencement of the lease: *Borthwick-Norton v. Collier*, [1950] 2 K.B. 594.
[4] *See, e.g.*, Lumley's "Public Health", 12th edn., Vol. 3, p. 2875 *et seq.*
[5] Vol. 3, p. 2875, and cases there cited, especially *Cook v. Montagu*
(1872), L.R. 7 Q.B. 418, and *Walford v. Hackney Board of Works* (1894),
43 W.R. 110.

where there are intermediate lessors, and the rent received by each is the same, the person ultimately receiving the rent is the owner, but where a lessor receives from his lessee more rent that he pays, he is the owner within the definition.

A rent collector or a trustee acting on behalf of the owner in the true sense may be an "owner" within the definition, but the amount that may be recovered from such an "owner" is limited to what he actually receives,[1] and a mere receiver who can do no more than pay money into the owner's bank account on his behalf, is not an owner within the definition.[2]

In those cases where the section empowers a notice to be served on the owner *or* the occupier[3] of named premises, the authority should exercise care in choosing the most appropriate person in the circumstances, in the light of the information available to them; if the person so chosen considers it would have been equitable for the other party to have been served, this may give him grounds for an appeal to the magistrates' court under s. 290 (3) (*f*) of the 1936 Act.

---

[1] Section 294 of the 1936 Act.
[2] *Bottomley v. Harrison*, [1952] 1 All E.R. 369.
[3] As, for example, in certain cases under s. 39 (1) of the 1936 Act.

APPENDIX

The respective powers of local and water authorities as a consequence of the Local Government Act, 1972, the Water Act, 1973, and the Control of Pollution Act, 1974.

Section of P.H.A. 1936	Authority having the powers givien by the section	Comment
14	R.W.A.	As re-written by W.A., s. 14 (1).
15	R.W.A.	As amended by W.A., Sched. 8,
16	—	Repealed.
17, 18, 19	R.W.A.	—
20	R.W.A.	As re-written by W.A. Sched. 8.
21	R.W.A. or L.A.	W.A., s. 14 (3).
22	R.W.A.	But *see* W.A., s. 14 (5).
23, 24	R.W.A.	—
25	L.A.	But *see* W.A., s. 14 (6) and (7).
26	—	Repealed.
27–31	R.W.A.	—
32	L.A.	(Sewer maps.)
33	R.W.A.	—
34	R.W.A.	As amended by W.A., s. 14 (4).
35	—	Repealed.
36	R.W.A.	—
37–39	L.A.	—
40	R.W.A. or L.A.	*See* p. 137
41	L.A.	—
42	R.W.A.	—
43–47	L.A.	—
48	R.W.A. or L.A.	*See* p. 170
49	L.A.	—
50	R.W.A. or L.A.	*See* p. 168
51–71	L.A.	ss. 61 and 62 amended by Health and Safety at Work, etc., Act 1974.

Section of Act	Authority having the powers given by the section	Comment
72–77		Repealed—but *see* C.P.A. 1974 *below*
78 *et seq.*	L.A.	(The later sections of the Act are not affected; but *see* below.)
Public Health (Drainage of Trade Premises) Act 1937	R.W.A.	As amended by C.P.A.
L.G. (M.P.) Act 1953, s. 13.	R.W.A.	(This is the section about "laterals".)
P.H.A., 1961; ss. 12–14, Part V, Sched. 2.	R.W.A.	—
Remainder of P.H.A. 1961	L.A.	—
C.P.A. 1974		
s. 12	C.A.	—
s. 13	C.A.	—
s. 14	D.A.	—
ss. 20 and 21	L.A.	—

ABBREVIATIONS

R.W.A.: regional water authority, including the Welsh National Water Development Authority.

L.A.: local authority, *i.e.*, the district council, London Borough council or the Common Council of the City of London.

C.A.: Collection authority. ⎱ *See* Control of Pollution Act,
D.A.: Disposal authority. ⎰ 1974, s. 30 (1).

W.A.: Water Act, 1973.

C.P.A.: Control of Pollution Act, 1974.

NOTE.—Although the local authority may not be responsible for the administration of specified sections, they may in practice carry out a function under arrangements made with the R.W.A. under section 15 of the Water Act 1973. Part XII of the 1936 Act applies so far as it relates to the sections transferred to R.W.A.s: *see* W.A., 1973, s. 14 (2).

Alphabetical
Index

Alphabetical Index

A

PAGE